THE RA MATERIAL

The Law of One
BOOK II

The Law of One
Book II

DON ELKINS ⚕ CARLA RUECKERT
JAMES ALLEN McCARTY

REDFeather™

MIND | BODY | SPIRIT

4880 Lower Valley Road, Atglen, PA 19310

First Printing 1982
ISBN: 978-0-924608-09-4

*3,000 copies of *The Law of One* were privately printed by L/L Research, Louisville, KY, before it was printed under the title *The Ra Material*.

Type set in Chaparral Pro

Book II
Softcover ISBN: 978-0-924608-09-4
Hardcover ISBN: 978-0-7643-6555-3
Box Set ISBN (Books I–V): 978-0-7643-6021-3
E-Book ISBN: 978-1-5073-0120-3

Printed in India

Updated Edition
10 9 8 7 6 5 4 3 2

Published by Red Feather Mind, Body, Spirit
An imprint of Schiffer Publishing, Ltd.
4880 Lower Valley Road
Atglen, PA 19310
Phone: (610) 593-1777; Fax: (610) 593-2002
E-mail: Info@schifferbooks.com
Web: www.redfeathermbs.com

For our complete selection of fine books on this and related subjects, please visit our website at www.schifferbooks.com. You may also write for a free catalog.

  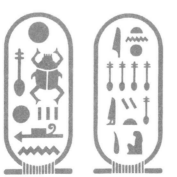 

FOREWORD

On January 15, 1981, our research group started receiving a communication from the social memory complex, Ra. From this communication precipitated the Law of One and some of the distortions of the Law of One.

The pages of this book contain an exact transcript, edited only to remove some personal material, of the communications received in Sessions 27 through 50 with Ra.

This material presupposes a point of view which we have developed in the course of many years' study of the UFO phenomenon. If you are not familiar with our previous work, a reading of our book, *Secrets of the UFO,* might prove helpful in understanding the present material. Book II of *The Law of One* builds very carefully on concepts received during the first 26 sessions with Ra, which were published as *The Law of One.* We encourage you to read *The Law of One* first if possible. Both books are available from us by mail.

Book II of *The Law of One* concentrates on the metaphysical principles which govern our spiritual evolution as we seek to understand and use the catalyst of our daily experiences. A more thorough examination of the energy centers of the body, and the connections between mind, body, and spirit, is carried out, building upon information received in the first 26 sessions. We learn more about Wanderers, the various densities, healing, and the many energy exchanges and blockages native to our illusion relating to experiences such as sex, illness, and meditation.

The first three sessions of Book II (27–29) may be difficult and confusing to anyone not familiar with the system of physics authored by Dewey B. Larson. Don't be discouraged, since Larsonian physics is far from well known. Just keep reading and by Session 30, you will be back on firm metaphysical ground. When you've finished Book II, go back and take another look at the first sessions. They'll seem a lot clearer. For those who may wish to study Larsonian physics, *The Structure of the Physical Universe* is a good book with which to begin.

On page 52, the questioner asks about an equation and does not use the classically correct form: in the physics of special relativity, the "c^2" term does not appear. Dr. Andrija Puharich received this form of the equation in his communication with The Nine and, therefore, we felt it appropriate to present it in this form, with the c^2 term included precisely as it had been received by Dr. Puharich.

The Ra contact continued for 106 sessions which were printed into four books in *The Law of One* series. They are available at your local bookstore, from Schiffer Publishing, or from us. If you wish to receive our quarterly newsletter, in which the best of our current channeling is published, please request that you be put on our mailing list.

L/L Research

DON ELKINS
CARLA L. RUECKERT
JIM MCCARTY

Louisville, Kentucky
March 17, 1982

Session 27,
February 21, 1981

RA: I am Ra. I greet you in the love and the light of the One Infinite Creator. I communicate now.

QUESTIONER: This session I thought we would start Book II of *The Law Of One*, which will focus on what we consider to be the only important aspect of our being. This, I assume, will be a much more difficult task than the first book. We want to focus on things that are not transient, and as questioner I may have difficulty at times.

When I do have this difficulty I may fall back on some transient questions simply because I will not be able to formulate what I really need, and I apologize for this. I will try my best to stay on the track and eliminate things of no value from the book if they do occur during my questioning.

The statement I will make to begin with is: In this density we tend to focus our minds on some transient condition or activity with little regard to its value or use as an aid or a tool for growth and understanding of the true and undistorted essence of the creation of which we are an integral part.

I will attempt, by starting at the beginning of creation, to establish an overview of ourselves in the creation, thereby arriving at a more informed viewpoint of what we consider to be reality. It is hoped that this will allow us to participate more effectively in the process of evolution.

I would like to start with definitions of words that we have been using that possibly we have not—and possibly cannot—understand totally, but since the first words that we use are intelligent infinity, I would like for you to define each of these words and give the definition of their combination.

RA: I am Ra. Your vibrations of mind complex indicate a query. However, your vibrational sound complex indicate a preference. Please restate.

QUESTIONER: Would you define the word intelligent in the context of intelligent infinity?

RA: I am Ra. We shall address the entire spectrum of this question before defining as requested. Your language, using vibrational sound complexes, can be at best an approximation of that which is closer to an understanding, if you will, of the nature of conscious thought.

Perceptions are not the same as sound vibration complexes and the attempt to define will therefore be a frustrating one for you, although we are happy to aid you within the limits of your sound vibration complexes.

To define intelligent apart from infinity is difficult, for these two vibration complexes equal one concept. It is much like attempting to divide your sound vibration concept, faith, into two parts. We shall attempt to aid you however.

QUESTIONER: It is not necessary to divide it. The definition of intelligent infinity is sufficient. Could you define that please?

RA: I am Ra. This is exponentially simpler and less confusing. There is unity. This unity is all that there is. This unity has a potential and kinetic. The potential is intelligent infinity. Tapping this potential will yield work. This work has been called by us, intelligent energy.

The nature of this work is dependent upon the particular distortion of free will which in turn is the nature of a particular intelligent energy of kinetic focus of the potential of unity or that which is all.

QUESTIONER: I would like to expand a little on the concept of work. In Newtonian physics the concept of work is the product of force and distance. I am assuming that the work of which you speak is a much broader term including possibly work in consciousness. Am I correct?

RA: I am Ra. As we use this term it is universal in application. Intelligent infinity has a rhythm or flow as of a giant heart beginning with the central sun as you would think or conceive of this, the presence of the flow inevitable as a tide of beingness without polarity, without finity; the vast and silent all beating outward, outward, focusing outward and inward until the focuses are complete. The intelligence or consciousness of foci have reached a state where their, shall we say, spiritual nature or mass calls them inward, inward, inward until all is coalesced. This is the rhythm of reality as you spoke.

QUESTIONER: Then I think I have extracted an important point from this in that in intelligent infinity we have work without polarity, or a potential difference does not have to exist. Is this correct?

RA: I am Ra. There is no difference, potential or kinetic, in unity.

The basic rhythms of intelligent infinity are totally without distortion of any kind. The rhythms are clothed in mystery, for they are being itself. From this undistorted unity, however, appears a potential in relation to intelligent energy.

In this way you may observe the term to be somewhat two-sided, one use of the term, that being as the undistorted unity, being without any kinetic or potential side. The other application of this term, which we use undifferentiatedly for lack of other terms in the sense of the vast potential tapped into by foci or focuses of energy, we call intelligent energy.

QUESTIONER: I understand that the first distortion of intelligent infinity is the distortion of what we call free will. Can you give me a definition of this distortion?

RA: I am Ra. In this distortion of the Law of One it is recognized that the Creator will know Itself.

QUESTIONER: Then am I correct in assuming that the Creator then grants for this knowing the concept of total freedom of choice in the ways of knowing? Am I correct?

RA: I am Ra. This is quite correct.

QUESTIONER: This then being the first distortion of the Law of One, which I am assuming is the Law of Intelligent Infinity, all other distortions which are the total experience of the creation spring from this. Is this correct?

RA: I am Ra. This is both correct and incorrect. In your illusion all experience springs from the Law of Free Will or the Way of Confusion. In another sense, which we are learning, the experiences are this distortion.

QUESTIONER: I will have to think about that and ask questions on it in the next session, so I will go on now to what you have given me as the second distortion which is the distortion of love.

Is this correct?

RA: I am Ra. This is correct.

QUESTIONER: I would like for you to define love in its sense as the second distortion.

RA: I am Ra. This must be defined against the background of

intelligent infinity or unity or the One Creator with the primal distortion of free will. The term Love then may be seen as the focus, the choice of attack, the type of energy of an extremely, shall we say, high order which causes intelligent energy to be formed from the potential of intelligent infinity in just such and such a way. This then may be seen to be an object rather than an activity by some of your peoples, and the principle of this extremely strong energy focus being worshipped as the Creator instead of unity or oneness from which all Loves emanate.

QUESTIONER: Is there a manifestation of love that we could call vibration?

RA: I am Ra. Again we reach semantic difficulties. The vibration or density of love or understanding is not a term used in the same sense as the second distortion, Love; the distortion Love being the great activator and primal co-Creator of various creations using intelligent infinity; the vibration love being that density in which those who have learned to do an activity called "loving" without significant distortion, then seek the ways of light or wisdom. Thus in vibratory sense love comes into light in the sense of the activity of unity in its free will. Love uses light and has the power to direct light in its distortions. Thus vibratory complexes recapitulate in reverse the creation in its unity, thus showing the rhythm or flow of the great heartbeat, if you will use this analogy.

QUESTIONER: I will make a statement that I have extracted from the physics of Dewey Larson which may or may not be close to what we are trying to explain. Larson says that all is motion which we can take as vibration, and that vibration is pure vibration and is not physical in any way or in any form or density, and the first product of that vibration is what we call the photon or particle of light. I am trying to make an analogy between this physical solution and the concept of love and light. Is this close to the concept of Love creating light?

RA: I am Ra. You are correct.

QUESTIONER: Then I will expand a bit more on this concept. We have the infinite vibration of Love which can occur, I am assuming, at varying frequencies.

I would assume that it begins at one basic frequency. Does this have any meaning?

RA: I am Ra. Each Love, as you term the prime movers, comes from one frequency, if you wish to use this term. This frequency is unity. We would perhaps liken it rather to a strength than a frequency, this strength being infinite, the finite qualities being chosen by the particular nature of this primal movement.

QUESTIONER: Then this vibration which is, for lack of better understanding, pure motion; it is pure love; it is nothing that is yet condensed, shall we say, to form any type of density of illusion. This Love then creates by this process of vibration a photon, as we call it, which is the basic particle of light. This photon then, by added vibrations and rotation, further condenses into particles of the densities we experience. Is this correct?

RA: I am Ra. This is correct.

QUESTIONER: Then this light which forms the densities has what we call color. This color is divided into seven categories. Can you tell me if there is a reason or explanation for these categories of color?

RA: I am Ra. This will be the last complete question of this session as this instrument is low on vital energy. We will answer briefly and then you may question further in subsequent sessions.

The nature of the vibratory patterns of your universe is dependent upon the configurations placed upon the original material or light by the focus or Love using Its intelligent energy to create a certain pattern of illusions or densities in order to satisfy Its own intelligent estimate of a method of knowing Itself. Thus the colors, as you call them, are as strait, or narrow, or necessary as is possible to express, given the will of Love.

There is further information which we shall be happy to share by answering your questions. However, we do not wish to deplete this instrument. Is there a short query necessary before we leave?

QUESTIONER: The only thing I need to know is if there is anything that we can do to make the instrument more comfortable or to help her or this contact?

RA: I am Ra. This instrument is slightly uncomfortable. Perhaps a simpler configuration of the body would be appropriate given the instrument's improving physical complex condition.

I am Ra. You are conscientious in your endeavors. We shall be with you. We leave you now in the love and in the light of the One

Infinite Creator. Rejoice, therefore, in the power and the peace of the One Infinite Creator. Adonai.

Session 28,
February 22, 1981

RA: I am Ra. I greet you in the love and the light of the Infinite Creator. I communicate now.

QUESTIONER: I may be backtracking a little today because I think that possibly we are at the most important part of what we are doing in trying to make it apparent how everything is one, how it comes from one intelligent infinity. This is difficult, so please bear with my errors in questioning.

The concept that I have right now of the process, using both what you have told me and some of Dewey Larson's material having to do with the physics of the process, is that intelligent infinity expands outward from all locations everywhere. It expands outward uniformly like the surface of a bubble or a balloon expanding outward from every point everywhere. It expands outward at what is called unit velocity or the velocity of light. This is Larson's idea of the progression of what he calls space/time. Is this concept correct?

RA: I am Ra. This concept is incorrect as is any concept of the one intelligent infinity. This concept is correct in the context of one particular Logos, or Love, or focus of this Creator which has chosen Its, shall we say, natural laws and ways of expressing them mathematically and otherwise.

The one undifferentiated intelligent infinity, unpolarized, full and whole, is the macrocosm of the mystery-clad being. We are messengers of the Law of One. Unity, at this approximation of understanding, cannot be specified by any physics but only become activated or potentiated intelligent infinity due to the catalyst of free will. This may be difficult to accept. However, the understandings we have to share begin and end in mystery.

QUESTIONER: Yesterday we had arrived at a point where we were considering colors of light. You said: "The nature of the vibratory patterns of your universe is dependent upon the configurations placed upon the original material or light by the focus or Love using Its intelligent energy to create a certain pattern of illusions or densities in order to satisfy Its own intelligent estimate of a method of knowing Itself." Then after this you said that there was more material that you would be happy to share, but we ran out of time. Could you give us further information on that?

RA: I am Ra. In discussing this information we then, shall we say, snap back into the particular methods of understanding or seeing that which the one, sound vibration complex, Dewey, offers; this being correct for the second meaning of intelligent infinity: the potential which then through catalyst forms the kinetic.

This information is a natural progression of inspection of the kinetic shape of your environment. You may understand each color or ray as being, as we had said, a very specific and accurate portion of intelligent energy's representation of intelligent infinity, each ray having been previously inspected in other regards .

This information may be of aid here. We speak now nonspecifically to increase the depth of your conceptualization of the nature of what is. The universe in which you live is recapitulation in each part of intelligent infinity. Thus you will see the same patterns repeated in physical and metaphysical areas; the rays or portions of light being, as you surmise, those areas of what you may call the physical illusion which rotate, vibrate, or are of a nature that may be, shall we say, counted or categorized in rotation manner in space/time as described by the one known as Dewey; some substances having various of the rays in a physical manifestation visible to the eye, this being apparent in the nature of your crystallized minerals which you count as precious, the ruby being red and so forth.

QUESTIONER: This light occurred as a consequence of vibration which is a consequence of Love. I am going to ask if that statement is correct?

RA: I am Ra. This statement is correct.

QUESTIONER: This light then can condense into material as we know it into our density, into all of our chemical elements because of rotations of the vibration at quantized units or intervals of angular velocity. Is this correct?

RA: I am Ra. This is quite correct.

QUESTIONER: Thank you. I am wondering, what is the catalyst or the activator of the rotation? What causes the rotation so that light condenses into our physical or chemical elements?

RA: I am Ra. It is necessary to consider the enabling function of the focus known as Love. This energy is of an ordering nature. It orders in a cumulative way from greater to lesser so that when Its universe, as you may call it, is complete, the manner of development of each detail is inherent in the living light and thus will develop in such and such a way; your own universe having been well studied in an empirical fashion by those you call your scientists and having been understood or visualized, shall we say, with greater accuracy by the understandings or visualizations of the one known as Dewey.

QUESTIONER: When does the individualization or the individualized portion of consciousness come into play? At what point does individualized consciousness take over working on the basic light?

RA: I am Ra. You remain carefully in the area of creation itself. In this process we must further confuse you by stating that the process by which free will acts upon potential intelligent infinity to become focused intelligent energy takes place without the space/time of which you are so aware as it is your continuum experience.

The experience or existence of space/time comes into being after the individuation process of Logos or Love has been completed and the physical universe, as you would call it, has coalesced or begun to draw inward while moving outward to the extent that that which you call your sun bodies have in their turn created timeless chaos coalescing into what you call planets, these vortices of intelligent energy spending a large amount of what you would call first density in a timeless state, the space/time realization being one of the learn/teachings of this density of beingness.

Thus we have difficulty answering your questions with regard to time and space and their relationship to the, what you would call, original creation which is not a part of space/time as you can understand it.

QUESTIONER: Thank you. Does a unit of consciousness, an individualized unit of consciousness, create a unit of the creation? I will give an example.

One individualized consciousness creates one galaxy of stars, the type that has many millions of stars in it. Does this happen?

RA: I am Ra. This can happen. The possibilities are infinite. Thus a Logos may create what you call a star system or it may be the Logos creating billions of star systems. This is the cause of the confusion in the term galaxy, for there are many different Logos entities or creations and we would call each, using your sound vibration complexes, a galaxy.

QUESTIONER: Let's take as an example the planet that we are on now and tell me how much of the creation was created by the same Logos that created this planet?

RA: I am Ra. This planetary Logos is a strong Logos creating approximately 250 billion of your star systems for Its creation. The, shall we say, laws or physical ways of this creation will remain, therefore, constant.

QUESTIONER: Then what you are saying is that the lenticular star system which we call a galaxy that we find ourselves in with approximately 250 billion other suns like our own was created by a single Logos. Is this correct?

RA: I am Ra. This is correct.

QUESTIONER: Since there are many individualized portions of consciousness in this lenticular galaxy, did this Logos then subdivide into more individualization of consciousness to create these consciousnesses?

RA: I am Ra. You are perceptive. This is also correct although an apparent paradox.

QUESTIONER: Could you tell me what you mean by an apparent paradox?

RA: I am Ra. It would seem that if one Logos creates the intelligent energy ways for a large system there would not be the necessity or possibility of the further sub-Logos differentiation. However, within limits, this is precisely the case, and it is perceptive that this has been seen.

QUESTIONER: Thank you. I'll call the lenticular galaxy that we are in the major galaxy just so we will not get mixed up in our terms. Does all the consciousness in individualized form that goes into what we are calling the major galaxy start out and go through all of the densities in order, one-two-three-four-five-six-seven and into the eighth, or are there some who start up higher in the rank so that there is always a mixture of intelligent consciousness in the galaxy?

RA: I am Ra. The latter is more nearly correct. In each beginning there is the beginning from infinite strength. Free will acts as a catalyst. Beings begin to form the universes. Consciousness then begins to have the potential to experience. The potentials of experience are created as a part of intelligent energy and are fixed before experience begins.

However, there is always, due to free will acting infinitely upon the creation, a great variation in initial responses to intelligent energy's potential. Thus almost immediately the foundations of the, shall we call it, hierarchical nature of beings begins to manifest as some portions of consciousness or awareness learn through experience in a much more efficient manner.

QUESTIONER: Is there any reason for some portions being much more efficient in learning?

RA: I am Ra. Is there any reason for some to learn more quickly than others? Look, if you wish, to the function of the will . . . the, shall we say, attraction to the upward spiraling line of light.

QUESTIONER: I am assuming that there are eight densities created when this major galaxy was created. Is this correct?

RA: I am Ra. This is basically correct. However, it is well to perceive that the eighth density functions also as the beginning density or first density, in its latter stages, of the next octave of densities.

QUESTIONER: Are you saying then that there are an infinite number of octaves of densities one through eight?

RA: I am Ra. We wish to establish that we are truly humble messengers of the Law of One. We can speak to you of our experiences and our understandings and teach/learn in limited ways. However, we cannot speak in firm knowledge of all the creations. We know only that they are infinite. We assume an infinite number of octaves.

However, it has been impressed upon us by our own teachers that there is a mystery-clad unity of creation in which all consciousness periodically coalesces and again begins. Thus we can only say we assume an infinite progression though we understand it to be cyclical in nature and, as we have said, clad in mystery.

QUESTIONER: Thank you. When this major galaxy is formed by the Logos, polarity then exists in a sense that we have electrical polarity. We do have electrical polarity existing at that time. Is that correct?

RA: I am Ra. I accept this as correct with the stipulation that what you term electrical be understood as not only the one, Larson, stipulated its meaning but also in what you would call the metaphysical sense.

QUESTIONER: Are you saying then that we have not only a polarity of electrical charge but also a polarity in consciousness at that time?

RA: I am Ra. This is correct. All is potentially available from the beginning of your physical space/time; it then being the function of consciousness complexes to begin to use the physical materials to gain experience to then polarize in a metaphysical sense. The potentials for this are not created by the experiencer but by intelligent energy.
This will be the last full question of this session due to our desire to foster this instrument as it slowly regains physical complex energy. May we ask if you have one or two questions we may answer shortly before we close?

QUESTIONER: I am assuming that the process of creation, after the original creation of the major galaxy, is continued by the further individualization of the consciousness of the Logos so that there are many, many portions of the individualized consciousness creating further items for experience all over the galaxy. Is this correct?

RA: I am Ra. This is correct, for within the, shall we say, guidelines or ways of the Logos, the sub-Logos may find various means of differentiating experiences without removing or adding to these ways.

QUESTIONER: Thank you. And since we are out of time I will ask if there is anything that we can do to make the instrument more comfortable or to help the contact?

RA: I am Ra. This instrument is well adjusted. You are conscientious.
I am Ra. I leave you, my friends, in the love and the light of the One Infinite Creator. Go forth then rejoicing in the power and the peace of the One Creator. Adonai.

Session 29,
February 23, 1981

RA: I am Ra. I greet you in the love and the light of the Infinite Creator. I communicate now.

QUESTIONER: Is our sun a sub-Logos or the physical manifestation of a sub-Logos?

RA: I am Ra. This is correct.

QUESTIONER: Then I am assuming that this sub-Logos created this planetary system in all of its densities. Is this correct?

RA: I am Ra. This is incorrect. The sub-Logos of your solar entity differentiated some experiential components within the patterns of intelligent energy set in motion by the Logos which created the basic conditions and vibratory rates consistent throughout your, what you have called, major galaxy.

QUESTIONER: Then is this sub-Logos which is our sun the same sub-Logos just manifesting in different parts through the galaxy, or is it all the stars in the galaxy?

RA: I am Ra. Please restate.

QUESTIONER: What I'm saying is that there are roughly 250 billion stars somewhat like ours in this major galaxy. Are they all part of the same sub-Logos?

RA: I am Ra. They are all part of the same Logos. Your solar system, as you would call it, is a manifestation somewhat and slightly different due to the presence of a sub-Logos.

QUESTIONER: Let me be sure I'm right then. Our sun is a sub-Logos of the Logos of the major galaxy?

RA: I am Ra. This is correct.

QUESTIONER: Are there any sub-sub-Logoi that are found in our planetary system that are "sub" to our sun?

RA: I am Ra. This is correct.

QUESTIONER: Would you give me an example of what I will call a sub-sub-Logos?

RA: I am Ra. One example is your mind/body/spirit complex.

QUESTIONER: Then every entity that exists would be some type of sub or sub-sub-Logos. Is that correct?

RA: I am Ra. This is correct down to the limits of any observation, for the entire creation is alive.

QUESTIONER: Then the planet which we walk upon here would be some form of sub-sub-Logos. Is this correct?

RA: I am Ra. A planetary entity is so named only as Logos if It is working in harmonic fashion with entities or mind/body complexes upon Its surface or within Its electromagnetic field.

QUESTIONER: Do the sub-Logoi such as our sun have a metaphysical polarity positive or negative as we have been using the term?

RA: I am Ra. As you use the term, this is not so. Entities through the level of planetary have the strength of intelligent infinity through the use of free will, going through the actions of beingness. The polarity is not thusly as you understand polarity. It is only when the planetary sphere begins harmonically interacting with mind/body complexes, and more especially mind/body/spirit complexes, that planetary spheres take on distortions due to the thought complexes of entities interacting with the planetary entity. The creation of the One Infinite Creator does not have the polarity you speak of.

QUESTIONER: Thank you. Yesterday you stated that planets in first density are in a timeless state to begin with. Can you tell me how the effect that we appreciate as time comes into being?

RA: I am Ra. We have just described to you the state of beingness of each Logos. The process by which space/time comes into continuum form is a function of the careful building, shall we say, of an entire or whole plan of vibratory rates, densities, and potentials. When this plan has coalesced in the thought complexes of Love, then the physical manifestations begin to appear; this first manifestation stage being awareness or consciousness.

At the point at which this coalescence is at the livingness or beingness point, the point or fountainhead of beginning, space/time then begins to unroll its scroll of livingness.

QUESTIONER: I believe that Love creates the vibration in space/time in order to form the photon. Is this correct?

RA: I am Ra. This is essentially correct.

QUESTIONER: Then the continued application of Love—I will assume that this is directed by a sub-Logos or a sub-sub-Logos—creates rotations of these vibrations which are in discrete units of angular velocity. This then creates chemical elements in our physical illusion and I will assume the elements in the nonphysical or other densities in the illusion. Is this correct?

RA: I am Ra. The Logos creates all densities. Your question was unclear. However, we shall state the Logos does create both the space/time densities and the accompanying time/space densities.

QUESTIONER: What I am assuming is that quantized incremental rotations of the vibrations show up as a material of these densities. Is this correct?

RA: I am Ra. This is essentially correct.

QUESTIONER: Then because of these rotations there is an inward motion of these particles which is opposite the direction of space/time progression as I understand it, and this inward progression then is seen by us as what we call gravity. Is this correct?

RA: I am Ra. This is incorrect.

QUESTIONER: Can you tell me how the gravity comes about?

RA: I am Ra. This that you speak of as gravity may be seen as the pressing towards the inner light/love, the seeking towards the spiral line of light which progresses towards the Creator. This is a manifestation of a spiritual event or condition of livingness.

QUESTIONER: The gravity that we know of on our moon is less than it is on our planet. Is there a metaphysical principle behind this that you could explain?

RA: I am Ra. The metaphysical and physical are inseparable. Thus that of which you spoke which attempts to explain this phenomenon is able to, shall we say, calculate the gravitational force of most objects due to the various physical aspects such as what you know of as mass. However, we felt it was necessary to indicate the corresponding and equally important metaphysical nature of gravity.

QUESTIONER: I sometimes have difficulty in getting a foothold into what I am looking for. I am trying to seek out the metaphysical principles, you might say, behind our physical illusion.

Could you give me an example of the amount of gravity in the third density conditions at the surface of the planet Venus? Would it be greater or less than Earth's?

RA: I am Ra. The gravity, shall we say, the attractive force which we also describe as the pressing outward force towards the Creator is greater spiritually upon the entity you call Venus due to the greater degree of success, shall we say, at seeking the Creator.

This point only becomes important when you consider that when all of creation in its infinity has reached a spiritual gravitational mass of sufficient nature, the entire creation infinitely coalesces; the light seeking and finding its source and thusly ending the creation and beginning a new creation much as you consider the black hole, as you call it, with its conditions of infinitely great mass at the zero point from which no light may be seen as it has been absorbed.

QUESTIONER: Then the black hole would be a point at which the environmental material has succeeded in uniting with unity or with the Creator? Is this correct?

RA: I am Ra. The black hole which manifests third density is the physical complex manifestation of this spiritual or metaphysical state. This is correct.

QUESTIONER: Then when our planet is fully into fourth density, will there be a greater gravity?

RA: I am Ra. There will be a greater spiritual gravity thus causing a denser illusion.

QUESTIONER: This denser illusion then I would assume increases gravitational acceleration above the 32 feet per second squared that we experience. Is this correct?

RA: I am Ra. Your entities do not have the instrumentation to measure spiritual gravity but only to observe a few of its extreme manifestations.

QUESTIONER: This I know, that we can't measure spiritual gravity, but I was just wondering if the physical effect could be measured as an increase in the gravitational constant? That was my question.

RA: I am Ra. The increase measurable by existing instrumentation would and will be statistical in nature only and not significant.

QUESTIONER: OK. As the creation is formed, as the atoms form as rotations of the vibration which is light, they coalesce in a certain manner sometimes. They produce a lattice structure which we call crystalline. I am guessing that because of the formation from intelligent energy of the precise crystalline structure that it is possible by some technique to tap intelligent energy and bring it into the physical illusion by working through the crystalline structure. Is this correct?

RA: I am Ra. This is correct only in so far as the crystalline physical structure is charged by a correspondingly crystallized or regularized or balanced mind/body/spirit complex.

QUESTIONER: I don't wish to get off on subjects of no importance, but it is difficult sometimes to see precisely in what direction to go. I would like to investigate a little bit more this idea of crystals, how they are used. I am assuming then from what you said that in order to use the crystal to tap intelligent energy, it is necessary to have a partially undistorted mind/body/spirit complex. Is this correct?

RA: I am Ra. This is specifically correct.

QUESTIONER: There must be a point at which the removal of distortion reaches the minimum for use of the crystal in tapping intelligent energy. Is this correct?

RA: I am Ra. This is correct only if it is understood, shall we say, that each mind/body/spirit complex has an unique such point.

QUESTIONER: Can you tell me why each mind/body/spirit complex has this unique point of distortion-ridding?

RA: I am Ra. Each mind/body/spirit complex is an unique portion of the One Creator.

QUESTIONER: Then you are saying that there is no single level of purity required to tap intelligent energy through crystals but there can be a wide variation in the amount of distortion that an entity may have, but each entity has to reach his particular point of what I might call energizing the ability. Is this right?

RA: I am Ra. This is incorrect. The necessity is for the mind/body/spirit complex to be of a certain balance, this balance thus enabling it to reach a set level of lack of distortion. The critical difficulties are unique for each mind/body/spirit complex due to the experiential distillations which in total are the, shall we say, violet-ray beingness of each such entity.

This balance is what is necessary for work to be done in seeking the gateway to intelligent infinity through the use of crystals or through any other use. No two mind/body/spirit crystallized natures are the same. The distortion requirements, vibrationally speaking, are set.

QUESTIONER: I see. Then if you are able to read the violet ray of an entity, to see that ray, is it possible to immediately determine whether the entity could use crystals to tap intelligent energy?

RA: I am Ra. It is possible for one of fifth density or above to do this.

QUESTIONER: Is it possible for you to tell me how an entity who has satisfactorily achieved the necessary violet ray qualification should use the crystal?

RA: I am Ra. The gateway to intelligent infinity is born of, shall we say, the sympathetic vibration in balanced state accompanying the will to serve, the will to seek.

QUESTIONER: Can you tell me precisely what the entity would do with the crystal to use it for the purpose of seeking the intelligent infinity?

RA: I am Ra. The use of the crystal in physical manifestation is that use wherein the entity of crystalline nature charges the regularized physical crystal with this seeking, thus enabling it to vibrate harmonically and also become the catalyst or gateway whereby intelligent infinity may thus become intelligent energy, this crystal serving as an analog of the violet ray of the mind/body/spirit in relatively undistorted form.

QUESTIONER: Is it possible for you to instruct us in the specific uses of crystals?

RA: I am Ra. It is possible. There are, we consider, things which are not efficacious to tell you due to possible infringement upon your free will. Entities of the Confederation have done this in the past. The uses of the crystal, as you know, include the uses for healing, for power, and even for the development of lifeforms. We feel that it is unwise to offer instruction at this time as your peoples have shown a tendency to use peaceful sources of power for disharmonious reasons.

QUESTIONER: Is it possible for you to give me an example of various planetary developments in what I would call a metaphysical sense having to do with the development of consciousness and its polarities throughout the galaxy? In other words I believe that some of these planets develop quite rapidly into higher density planets and some take longer times. Can you give me some idea of that development?

RA: I am Ra. This will be the final full query of this session.

The particular Logos of your major galaxy has used a large portion of Its coalesced material to reflect the beingness of the Creator. In this way there is much of your galactic system which does not have the progression of which you speak but dwells spiritually as a portion of the Logos. Of those entities upon which consciousness dwells there is, as you surmise, a variety of time/space periods during which the higher densities of experience are attained by consciousness.

Is there any short query further before we close?

QUESTIONER: Is there anything that we can do to make the instrument more comfortable or to improve the contact?

RA: I am Ra. You are conscientious. The entity is well aligned.

I am Ra. I leave you now in the love and the light of the One Infinite Creator. Go forth, therefore, rejoicing in the power and the peace of the One Infinite Creator. Adonai.

Session 30,
February 24, 1981

RA: I am Ra. I greet you in the love and in the light of the One Infinite Creator. We communicate now.

QUESTIONER: I am going to make a statement and then let you correct it if I have made any errors. This is the statement: Creation is a single entity or unity. If only a single entity exists, then the only concept of service is the concept of service to self. If this single entity subdivides, then the concept of service of one of its parts to one of its other parts is born. From this springs the equality of service to self or to others. It would seem that as the Logos subdivided, parts would select each orientation. As individualized entities emerge in space/time then I would assume that they have polarity. Is this statement correct?

RA: I am Ra. This statement is quite perceptive and correct until the final phrase in which we note that the polarities begin to be explored only at the point when a third density entity becomes aware of the possibility of choice between the concept or distortion of service to self or service to others. This marks the end of what you may call the unself-conscious or innocent phase of conscious awareness.

QUESTIONER: Thank you. Would you define mind, body, and spirit separately?

RA: I am Ra. These terms are all simplistic descriptive terms which equal a complex of energy focuses; the body, as you call it, being the material of the density which you experience at a given space/time or time/space; this complex of materials being available for distortions of what you would call physical manifestation.

The mind is a complex which reflects the inpourings of the spirit and the up-pourings of the body complex. It contains what you know as feelings, emotions, and intellectual thoughts in its more conscious complexities. Moving further down the tree of mind we see the intuition which is of the nature of the mind more in contact or in tune with the total beingness complex. Moving down to the roots of mind we find the progression of consciousness which gradually turns from the personal to the racial memory, to the cosmic influxes, and thus becomes a direct contactor of that shuttle which we call the spirit complex.

This spirit complex is the channel whereby the inpourings from all of the various universal, planetary, and personal inpourings may be funneled into the roots of consciousness and whereby consciousness may be funneled to the gateway of intelligent infinity through the balanced intelligent energy of body and mind.

You will see by this series of definitive statements that mind, body, and spirit are inextricably intertwined and cannot continue, one without the other. Thus we refer to the mind/body/spirit complex rather than attempting to deal with them separately, for the work, shall we say, that you do during your experiences is done through the interaction of these three components, not through any one.

QUESTIONER: Upon our physical death, as we call it, from this particular density and this particular incarnative experience, we lose this chemical body. Immediately after the loss of this chemical body do we maintain a different type of body? Is there still a mind/body/spirit complex at that point?

RA: I am Ra. This is correct. The mind/body/spirit complex is quite intact; the physical body complex you now associate with the term body being but manifestation of a more dense and intelligently informed and powerful body complex.

QUESTIONER: Is there any loss to the mind or spirit after this transition which we call death or any impairment of either because of the loss of this chemical body which we now have?

RA: I am Ra. In your terms there is a great loss of mind complex due to the fact that much of the activity of the mental nature of which you are aware during the experience of this space/time continuum is as much of a surface illusion as is the chemical body complex.

In other terms nothing whatever of importance is lost; the character or, shall we say, pure distillation of emotions and biases or distortions and wisdoms, if you will, becoming obvious for the first time, shall we say; these pure emotions and wisdoms and bias/distortions being, for the most part, either ignored or underestimated during physical life experience.

In terms of the spiritual, this channel is then much opened due to the lack of necessity for the forgetting characteristic of third density.

QUESTIONER: I would like to know how the mind/body/spirit

complexes originate, going as far back as necessary. How does the origination occur? Do they originate by spirit forming mind and mind forming body? Can you tell me this?

RA: I am Ra. We ask you to consider that you are attempting to trace evolution. This evolution is as we have previously described, the consciousness being first, in first density, without movement, a random thing. Whether you may call this mind or body complex is a semantic problem. We call it mind/body complex recognizing always that in the simplest iota of this complex exists in its entirety the One Infinite Creator; this mind/body complex then in second density discovering the growing and turning towards the light, thus awakening what you may call the spirit complex, that which intensifies the upward spiraling towards the love and light of the Infinite Creator.

The addition of this spirit complex, though apparent rather than real, it having existed potentially from the beginning of space/time, perfects itself by graduation into third density. When the mind/body/spirit complex becomes aware of the possibility of service to self or other-self, then the mind/body/spirit complex is activated.

QUESTIONER: Thank you. I don't wish to cover ground that we have covered before but it sometimes is helpful to restate these concepts for complete clarity since words are a poor tool for what we do.

Just as a passing point, I was wondering—on this planet during the second density, I believe there was habitation during the same space/time of bipedal entities and what we call the dinosaurs. Is this correct?

RA: I am Ra. This is correct.

QUESTIONER: These two types of entities seemed to be very incompatible, you might say, with each other. I don't know, but can you tell me the reason for both types of entities inhabiting the same space/time?

RA: I am Ra. Consider the workings of free will as applied to evolution. There are paths that the mind/body complex follows in an attempt to survive, to reproduce, and to seek in its fashion that which is unconsciously felt as the potential for growth; these two arenas or paths of development being two among many.

QUESTIONER: In second density the concept of bisexual reproduction first originates. Is this correct?

RA: I am Ra. This is correct.

QUESTIONER: Can you tell me the philosophy behind this method of propagation of the bodily complex?

RA: I am Ra. The second density is one in which the groundwork is being laid for third density work. In this way it may be seen that the basic mechanism of reproduction capitulates into a vast potential in third density for service to other-self and to self; this being not only by the functions of energy transfer, but also by the various services performed due to the close contact of those who are, shall we say, magnetically attracted, one to the other; these entities thus having the opportunities for many types of service which would be unavailable to the independent entity.

QUESTIONER: Was the basic reason for this to increase the opportunity of the experience of the One Creator?

RA: I am Ra. This is not merely correct but is the key to that which occurs in all densities.

QUESTIONER: Does the process of bisexual reproduction or the philosophy of it play a part in the spiritual growth of second density entities?

RA: I am Ra. In isolated instances this is so due to efficient perceptions upon the part of entities or species. For the greater part, by far, this is not the case in second density, the spiritual potentials being those of third density.

QUESTIONER: Thank you. Can you give me a brief history of the metaphysical principles of the development of each of our planets that surround our sun, their function with respect to the evolution of beings?

RA: I am Ra. We shall give you a metaphysical description only of those planets upon which individual mind/body/spirit complexes have been, are, or shall be experienced. You may understand the other spheres to be a part of the Logos.

We take the one known as Venus. This planetary sphere was one of rapid evolution. It is our native earth and the rapidity of the progress of the mind/body/spirit complexes upon its surface was due to harmonious interaction.

Upon the entity known to you as Mars, as you have already discussed, this entity was stopped in mid-third density, thus being unable to continue in progression due to the lack of hospitable conditions upon the surface. This planet shall be undergoing healing for some of your space/time millennia.

The planet which you dwell upon has a metaphysical history well known to you and you may ask about it if you wish. However, we have spoken to a great degree upon this subject.

The planet known as Saturn has a great affinity for the infinite intelligence and thus it has been dwelled upon in its magnetic fields of time/space by those who wish to protect your system.

The planetary entity known to you as Uranus is slowly moving through the first density and has the potential of moving through all densities.

QUESTIONER: Thank you. You stated yesterday that much of this major galactic system dwells spiritually as a part of the Logos. Do you mean that near the center of this major galactic system that the stars there do not have planetary systems? Is this correct?

RA: I am Ra. This is incorrect. The Logos has distributed Itself throughout your galactic system. However, the time/space continua of some of your more central sun systems are much further advanced.

QUESTIONER: Well then, could you generally say that as you get closer to the center of this major system that there is a greater spiritual density or spiritual quality in that area?

RA: I am Ra. This will be the last full question of this session as this instrument is somewhat uncomfortable. We do not wish to deplete the instrument.

The spiritual density or mass of those more towards the center of your galaxy is known. However, this is due simply to the varying timelessness states during which the planetary spheres may coalesce, this process of space/time beginnings occurring earlier, shall we say, as you approach the center of the galactic spiral.

QUESTIONER: Is there anything that we can do to make the instrument more comfortable or to improve the contact?

RA: This instrument is well balanced and the contact is as it should be. This instrument has certain difficulties of a distortion you would call the muscular spasm, thus making the motionless position uncomfortable. Thus we leave the instrument.

I am Ra. You are doing well, my friends. I leave you in the love and the light of the One Infinite Creator. Go forth, then, rejoicing in the power and the peace of the One Creator. Adonai.

Session 31,
February 25, 1981

RA: I am Ra. I greet you in the love and in the light of the One Infinite Creator. We communicate now.

QUESTIONER: I have a question that the instrument has asked me to ask. It reads: You speak of various types of energy blockages and transfers, positive and negative, that may take place due to participation in our sexual reproductive complex of actions. Could you please explain these blockages and energy transfers with emphasis upon what an individual who is seeking to be in accordance with the Law of One may positively do in this area? Is it possible for you to answer this question?

RA: I am Ra. It is partially possible, given the background we have laid. This is properly a more advanced question. Due to the specificity of the question we may give a general answer.

The first energy transfer is red ray. It is a random transfer having to do only with your reproductive system.

The orange- and the yellow-ray attempts to have sexual intercourse create, firstly, a blockage if only one entity vibrates in this area, thus causing the entity vibrating sexually in this area to have a never-ending appetite for this activity. What these vibratory levels are seeking is green ray activity. There is the possibility of orange or yellow ray energy transfer; this being polarizing towards the negative: one being seen as object rather than other-self; the other seeing itself as plunderer or master of the situation.

In green ray there are two possibilities. Firstly, if both vibrate in green ray there will be a mutually strengthening energy transfer, the negative or female, as you call it, drawing the energy from the roots of the beingness through the energy centers, thus being physically revitalized; the positive, or male polarity, as it is deemed in your illusion, finding in its energy transfer an inspiration which satisfies and feeds the spirit portion of the body/mind/spirit complex, thus both being polarized and releasing the excess of that which each has in abundance by nature of intelligent energy, that is, negative/intuitive, positive/physical energies as you may call them; this energy transfer being blocked only if one or both entities have fear of possession or of being possessed, of desiring possession or desiring being possessed.

The other green-ray possibility is that of one entity offering green-ray energy, the other not offering energy of the universal love energy, this resulting in a blockage of energy for the one not green ray thus increasing frustration or appetite; the green ray being polarizing slightly towards service to others.

The blue ray energy transfer is somewhat rare among your people at this time but is of great aid due to energy transfers involved in becoming able to express the self without reservation or fear.

The indigo-ray transfer is extremely rare among your people. This is the sacramental portion of the body complex whereby contact may be made through violet ray with intelligent infinity. No blockages may occur at these latter two levels due to the fact that if both entities are not ready for this energy it is not visible and neither transfer nor blockage may take place. It is as though the distributor were removed from a powerful engine.

QUESTIONER: Could you define sexual energy transfer and expand upon its meaning, please?

RA: I am Ra. Energy transfer implies the release of potential energies across, shall we say, a potentiated space. The sexual energy transfers occur due to the polarizations of two mind/body/spirit complexes, each of which have some potential difference one to the other. The nature of the transfer of energy or of the blockage of this energy is then a function of the interaction of these two potentials. In the cases where transfer takes place, you may liken this to a circuit being closed. You may also see this activity, as all experiential activities, as the Creator experiencing Itself.

QUESTIONER: Could this then be the primal mechanism for the Creator to experience Itself?

RA: I am Ra. This is not a proper term. Perhaps the adjectives would be "one appropriate" way of the Creator knowing Itself, for in each interaction, no matter what the distortion, the Creator is experiencing Itself. The bisexual knowing of the Creator by Itself has the potential for two advantages.

Firstly, in the green-ray-activated being there is the potential for a direct and simple analog of what you may call joy, the spiritual or metaphysical nature which exists in intelligent energy. This is a great aid to comprehension of a truer nature of beingness. The other potential advantage of bisexual reproductive acts is the possibility of a sacramental understanding or connection, shall we say, with the gateway to intelligent infinity, for with appropriate preparation, work in what you may call magic may be done and experiences of intelligent infinity may be had.

The positively oriented individuals concentrating upon this method of reaching intelligent infinity, then, through the seeking or the act of will, are able to direct this infinite intelligence to the work these entities desire to do, whether it be knowledge of service or ability to heal or whatever service to others is desired.

These are two advantages of this particular method of the Creator experiencing Itself. As we have said before, the corollary of the strength of this particular energy transfer is that it opens the door, shall we say, to the individual mind/body/spirit complexes' desire to serve in an infinite number of ways an other-self, thus polarizing towards positive.

QUESTIONER: Can you expand somewhat on the concept that this action not only allows the Creator to know Itself better but also creates, in our density, an offspring or makes available the pathway for another entity to enter this density?

RA: I am Ra. As we have previously said, the sexual energy transfers include the red-ray transfer which is random and which is a function of the second-density attempt to grow, to survive, shall we say. This is a proper function of the sexual interaction. The offspring, as you call the incarnated entity, takes on the mind/body complex opportunity offered by this random act or event called the fertilization of egg by seed which causes an entity to have the opportunity to then enter this density as an incarnate entity.

This gives the two who were engaged in this bisexual reproductive energy transfer the potential for great service in this area of the nurturing of the small-experienced entity as it gains in experience.

It shall be of interest at this point to note that there is always the possibility of using these opportunities to polarize towards the negative, and this has been aided by the gradual building up over many thousands of your years of social complex distortions which create a tendency towards confusion, shall we say, or baffling of the service-to-others aspect of this energy transfer and subsequent opportunities for service to other selves.

QUESTIONER: If a sexual energy transfer occurs in green ray—and

I am assuming in this case that there is no red ray energy transfer—does this mean it is impossible for this particular transfer to include fertilization and the birthing of an entity?

RA: I am Ra. This is incorrect. There is always the red-ray energy transfer due to the nature of the body complex. The random result of this energy transfer will be as it will be, as a function of the possibility of fertilization at a given time in a given pairing of entities each entity being undistorted in any vital sense by the yellow or orange ray energies; thus the gift, shall we say, being given freely, no payment being requested either of the body, of the mind, or of the spirit. The green ray is one of complete universality of love. This is a giving without expectation of return.

QUESTIONER: I was wondering if there was some principle behind the fact that a sexual union does not necessarily lead to fertilization. I'm not interested in the chemical or physical principles of it. I'm interested in whether or not there is some metaphysical principle that leads to the couple having a child or not, or is it purely random?

RA: I am Ra. This is random within certain limits. If an entity has reached the seniority whereby it chooses the basic structure of the life experience, this entity may then choose to incarnate in a physical complex which is not capable of reproduction. Thus we find some entities which have chosen to be unfertile. Other entities, through free will, make use of various devices to insure nonfertility. Except for these conditions, the condition is random.

QUESTIONER: Thank you. In the previous material you mentioned "magnetic attraction." Would you define and expand upon that term?

RA: I am Ra. We used the term to indicate that in your bisexual natures there is that which is of polarity. This polarity may be seen to be variable according to the, shall we say, male/female polarization of each entity, be each entity biologically male or female. Thus you may see the magnetism which two entities with the appropriate balance, male/female versus female/male polarity, meeting and thus feeling the attraction which polarized forces will exert, one upon the other.

This is the strength of the bisexual mechanism. It does not take an act of will to decide to feel attraction for one who is oppositely polarized sexually. It will occur in an inevitable sense, giving the free flow of energy a proper, shall we say, avenue. This avenue may be blocked by some distortion toward a belief/condition stating to the entity that this attraction is not desired. However, the basic mechanism functions as simply as would, shall we say, the magnet and the iron.

QUESTIONER: We have what seems to be an increasing number of entities incarnate here now who have what is called a homosexual orientation. Could you explain and expand upon that concept?

RA: I am Ra. Entities of this condition experience a great deal of distortion due to the fact that they have experienced many incarnations as biological male and as biological female. This would not suggest what you call homosexuality in an active phase were it not for the difficult vibratory condition of your planetary sphere. There is what you may call great aura infringement among your crowded urban areas in your more populous countries, as you call portions of your planetary surface. Under these conditions the confusions will occur.

QUESTIONER: Why does density of population create these confusions?

RA: I am Ra. The bisexual reproductive urge has as its goal, not only the simple reproductive function, but more especially the desire to serve others being awakened by this activity.

In an over-crowded situation where each mind/body/spirit complex is under constant bombardment from other-selves it is understandable that those who are especially sensitive would not feel the desire to be of service to other-selves. This would also increase the probability of a lack of desire or a blockage of the red ray reproductive energy.

In an uncrowded atmosphere this same entity would, through the stimulus of feeling the solitude about it, then have much more desire to seek out someone to whom it may be of service, thus regularizing the sexual reproductive function.

QUESTIONER: Roughly how many previous incarnations would a male entity in this incarnation have had to have had in the past as a female to have a highly homosexual orientation in this incarnation?

RA: I am Ra. If an entity has had roughly 65 percent of its incarnations in the sexual/biological body complex, the opposite polarity to its present body complex, this entity is vulnerable to infringement of your urban areas and may perhaps become of what you call an homosexual nature.

It is to be noted at this juncture that although it is much more difficult, it is possible in this type of association for an entity to be of great service to another in fidelity and sincere green ray love of a nonsexual nature thus adjusting or lessening the distortions of its sexual impairment.

QUESTIONER: Is there an imprint occurring on the DNA coding of an entity so that sexual biases are imprinted due to early sexual experiences?

RA: I am Ra. This is partially correct. Due to the nature of solitary sexual experiences, it is in most cases unlikely that what you call masturbation has an imprinting effect upon later experiences.

This is similarly true with some of the encounters which might be seen as homosexual among those of this age group. These are often, instead, innocent exercises in curiosity.

However, it is quite accurate that the first experience in which the mind/body/spirit complex is intensely involved will indeed imprint upon the entity for that life experience a set of preferences.

QUESTIONER: Does the Orion group use this as a gateway to impress upon entities preferences which could be of a negative polarization?

RA: I am Ra. Just as we of the Confederation attempt to beam our love and light whenever given the opportunity, including sexual opportunities, so the Orion group will use an opportunity if it is negatively oriented or if the individual is negatively oriented.

QUESTIONER: Is there any emotional bias that has nothing to do with male/female sexual polarity that can create sexual energy buildup in an entity?

RA: I am Ra. The sexual energy buildup is extremely unlikely to occur without sexual bias upon the part of the entity. Perhaps we did not understand your question, but it seems obvious that it would take an entity with the potential for sexual activity to experience a sexual energy buildup.

QUESTIONER: I was thinking more of the possibility of the Orion group influencing certain members of the Third Reich who I have read reports of having sexual gratification from the observation of the gassing and killing of entities in the gas chambers.

RA: I am Ra. We shall repeat these entities had the potential for sexual energy buildup. The choice of stimulus is certainly the choice of the entity. In the case of which you speak, these entities were strongly polarized orange ray, thus finding the energy blockage of power over others, the putting to death being the ultimate power over others; this then being expressed in a sexual manner, though solitary.

In this case the desire would continue unabated and be virtually unquenchable.

You will find, if you observe the entire spectrum of sexual practices among your peoples, that there are those who experience such gratification from domination over others either from rape or from other means of domination. In each case this is an example of energy blockage which is sexual in its nature.

QUESTIONER: Would the Orion group be able, then, to impress on entities this orange ray effect? Is this the way that this came about? If we go back to the beginning of third density there must be a primal cause of this.

RA: I am Ra. The cause of this is not Orion. It is the free choice of your peoples. This is somewhat difficult to explain. We shall attempt.

The sexual energy transfers and blockages are more a manifestation or example of that which is more fundamental than the other way about. Therefore, as your peoples became open to the concepts of bellicosity and the greed of ownership, these various distortions then began to filter down through the tree of mind into body complex expressions, the sexual expression being basic to that complex. Thus these sexual energy blockages, though Orion influenced and intensified, are basically the product of the beingness chosen freely by your peoples.

This will be the final question unless we may speak further upon this question to clarify, or answer any short queries before we close.

QUESTIONER: I just need to know then if this works through the racial memory and infects the entire population in some way?

RA: I am Ra. The racial memory contains all that has been

experienced. Thus there is some, shall we say, contamination even of the sexual, this showing mostly in your own culture as the various predispositions to adversary relationships, or, as you call them, marriages, rather than the free giving one to another in the love and the light of the Infinite Creator.

QUESTIONER: That was precisely the point that I was trying to make. Thank you very much. I do not wish to overtire the instrument, so I will just ask if there is anything that we can do to make the instrument more comfortable or to improve the contact?

RA: I am Ra. Please be aware that this instrument is somewhat fatigued. The channel is very clear. However, we find the vital energy low. We do not wish to deplete the instrument. However, there is, shall we say, an energy exchange that we feel an honor/duty to offer when this instrument opens itself. Therefore, counsel we this instrument to attempt to assess the vital energies carefully before offering itself as open channel.

All is well. You are conscientious.

I am Ra. I leave this instrument and you in the love and in the light of the One Infinite Creator. Go forth, then, rejoicing in the power and the peace of the One Creator. Adonai.

Session 32,
February 27, 1981

RA: I am Ra. I greet you in the love and the light of the One Infinite Creator. We communicate now.

QUESTIONER: We will now continue with the material from the day before yesterday. The subject is how sexual polarity acts as a catalyst in evolution and how to best make use of this catalyst. Going back to that material, I will fill in a few gaps that we possibly do not understand too well at this point.

Can you tell me the difference between orange- and yellow-ray activation? I am going to work up from the red ray right on through the violet. We have covered red ray, so I would like to ask now what the difference is between yellow- and orange-ray activation?

RA: I am Ra. The orange ray is that influence or vibratory pattern wherein the mind/body/spirit expresses its power on an individual basis. Thus power over individuals may be seen to be orange ray. This ray has been quite intense among your peoples on an individual basis. You may see in this ray the treating of other-selves as non-entities, slaves, or chattel, thus giving other-selves no status whatever.

The yellow ray is a focal and very powerful ray and concerns the entity in relation to, shall we say, groups, societies, or large numbers of mind/body/spirit complexes. This orange—we correct ourselves— this yellow-ray vibration is at the heart of bellicose actions in which one group of entities feels the necessity and right of dominating other groups of entities and bending their wills to the wills of the masters. The negative path, as you would call it, uses a combination of the yellow ray and the orange ray in its polarization patterns. These rays, used in a dedicated fashion, will bring about a contact with intelligent infinity. The usual nature of sexual interaction, if one is yellow or orange in primary vibratory patterns, is one of blockage and then insatiable hunger due to the blockage. When there are two selves vibrating in this area the potential for polarization through the sexual interaction is begun, one entity experiencing the pleasure of humiliation and slavery or bondage, the other experiencing the pleasure of mastery and control over another entity. This way a sexual energy transfer of a negative polarity is experienced.

QUESTIONER: From the material that you transmitted February 17th you stated: "In third ray there are two possibilities. Firstly, if both vibrate in third ray there will be a mutually strengthening energy transfer." What color is third ray in this material?

RA: I am Ra. The ray we were speaking of in that material should be properly the green ray or fourth ray.

QUESTIONER: So I should change that third to fourth or green?

RA: This is correct. Please continue to scan for errors having to do with numbering, as you call them, as this concept is foreign to us and we must translate, if you will, when using numbers. This is an ongoing weakness of this contact due to the difference between our ways and yours. Your aid is appreciated.

QUESTIONER: Thank you. I believe for the time being we have amply covered green ray, so I am going to skip over green ray and go to blue ray. Could you tell me the difference that occurs between green ray and blue ray with the emphasis on blue ray?

RA: I am Ra. With the green ray transfer of energy you now come to the great turning point sexually as well as in each other mode of experience. The green ray may then be turned outward, the entity then giving rather than receiving. The first giving beyond green ray is the giving of acceptance or freedom, thus allowing the recipient of blue ray energy transfer the opportunity for a feeling of being accepted, thus freeing that other-self to express itself to the giver of this ray. It will be noted that once green ray energy transfer has been achieved by two mind/body/spirits in mating, the further rays are available without both entities having the necessity to progress equally. Thus a blue-ray-vibrating entity or indigo-ray-vibrating entity whose other ray vibrations are clear may share that energy with the green-ray other-self, thus acting as catalyst for the continued learn/teaching of the other-self. Until an other-self reaches green ray, such energy transfer through the rays is not possible.

QUESTIONER: What is the difference between indigo and blue ray transfer?

RA: I am Ra. The indigo ray is the ray of, shall we say, awareness of the Creator as self; thus one whose indigo ray vibrations have been activated can offer the energy transfer of Creator to Creator. This is the beginning of the sacramental nature of what you call your bisexual reproductive act. It is unique in bearing the allness, the wholeness, the unity in its offering to other-self.

QUESTIONER: What is the difference between violet ray and the others?

RA: I am Ra. The violet ray, just as the red ray, is constant in the sexual experience. Its experience by other-self may be distorted or completely ignored or not apprehended by other-self. However, the violet ray, being the sum and substance of the mind/body/spirit complex, surrounds and informs any action by a mind/body/spirit complex.

QUESTIONER: Do the energy transfers of this nature occur in the fifth, sixth, and seventh density—all the rays?

RA: I am Ra. The rays, as you understand them, have such a different meaning in the next density and the next and so forth that we must answer your query in the negative. Energy transfers only take place in fourth, fifth, and sixth densities. These are still of what you would call a polarized nature. However, due to the ability of these densities to see the harmonies between individuals, these entities choose those mates which are harmonious, thus allowing constant transfer of energy and the propagation of the body complexes which each density uses. The process is different in the fifth and the sixth density than you may understand it. However, it is in these cases still based upon polarity. In the seventh density there is not this particular energy exchange as it is unnecessary to recycle body complexes.

QUESTIONER: I am assuming we have on Earth today and have had in the past fourth-, fifth-, and sixth-density Wanderers. As they come into incarnation in the physical of this density for a period as a Wanderer, what types of polarizations with respect to these various rays do they find affecting them?

RA: I am Ra. I believe I grasp the thrust of your query. Please ask further if this answer is not sufficient.

Fourth-density Wanderers, of which there are not many, will tend to choose those entities which seem to be full of love or in need of love. There is the great possibility/probability of entities making errors in judgment due to the compassion with which other-selves are viewed.

The fifth-density Wanderer is one who is not tremendously affected by the stimulus of the various rays of other-self, and in its own way offers itself when a need is seen. Such entities are not likely to engage in the, shall we say, custom of your peoples called marriage and are very likely to feel an aversion to childbearing and child raising due to the awareness of the impropriety of the planetary vibrations relative to the harmonious vibrations of the density of light.

The sixth density, whose means of propagation you may liken to what you call fusion, is likely to refrain, to a great extent, from the bisexual reproductive programming of the bodily complex and instead seek out those with whom the sexual energy transfer is of the complete fusion nature insofar as this is possible in manifestation in third density.

QUESTIONER: Can you expand a little bit on what you mean by "complete fusion nature"?

RA: I am Ra. The entire creation is of the One Creator. Thus the division of sexual activity into simply that of the bodily complex is an artificial division, all things thusly being seen as sexual equally, the mind, the body, and the spirit; all of which are part of the polarity of the entity. Thus sexual fusion may be seen with or without what you may call sexual intercourse to be the complete melding of the mind, the body, and the spirit in what feels to be a constant orgasm, shall we say, of joy and delight each in the other's beingness.

QUESTIONER: Would many Wanderers of these densities have considerable problems with respect to incarnation in the third density because of this different orientation?

RA: I am Ra. The possibility/probability of such problems, as you call them, due to sixth density incarnating in third is rather large. It is not necessarily a problem if you would call it thusly. It depends upon the unique orientation of each mind/body/spirit complex having this situation or placement of vibratory relativities.

QUESTIONER: Can you give me an idea how the different colors . . . This is a difficult question to ask. I'm having trouble finding any words. What I'm trying to get at is how the different colors originate as the functions for the different expressions in consciousness? I don't know if this question is sufficient.

RA: I am Ra. This question is sufficiently clear for us to attempt explanation of what, as you have observed, is not easily grasped material for the intellectual mind. The nature of vibration is such that it may be seen as having mathematically strait or narrow steps. These steps may be seen as having boundaries. Within each boundary there are infinite gradations of vibration or color. However, as one approaches a boundary, an effort must be made to cross that boundary. These colors are a simplistic way of expressing the boundary divisions of your density. There is also the time/space analogy which may be seen as the color itself in a modified aspect.

QUESTIONER: Thank you. Is it possible for an entity in third-density physical to vary across the entire band of colors or is the entity pretty well zeroed in on one color?

RA: I am Ra. This will be the last full question of this working. Please restate for clarity.

QUESTIONER: I meant was it possible for a green-ray person who is primarily of green-ray activation to vary on both sides of the green ray in a large or a small amount in regards to energy activation, or is he primarily green ray?

RA: I am Ra. We grasp the newness of material requested by you. It was unclear, for we thought we had covered this material. The portion covered is this: the green-ray activation is always vulnerable to the yellow or orange ray of possession, this being largely yellow ray but often coming into orange ray. Fear of possession, desire for possession, fear of being possessed, desire to be possessed: these are the distortions which will cause the deactivation of green-ray energy transfer.

The new material is this: once the green ray has been achieved, the ability of the entity to enter blue ray is immediate and is only awaiting the efforts of the individual. The indigo ray is opened only through considerable discipline and practice largely having to do with acceptance of self, not only as the polarized and balanced self but as the Creator, as an entity of infinite worth. This will begin to activate the indigo ray.

QUESTIONER: Thank you.

RA: I am Ra. Do you have any brief queries before we close?

QUESTIONER: I think that anything I have would be too long, so I will just ask if there is anything that we can do to make the instrument more comfortable or to make the contact better?

RA: I am Ra. All is well. We caution not only this instrument but each to look well to the vital energies necessary for nondepletion of the instrument and the contact level. You are most conscientious, my friends. We shall be with you. I leave you now in the love and in the light of the One Infinite Creator. Go forth, then, rejoicing in the power and the peace of the One Infinite Creator. Adonai.

Session 33,
March 1, 1981

RA: I am Ra. I greet you in the love and in the light of the One Infinite Creator. I communicate now.

QUESTIONER: In our last session you said that each of us in these sessions should look well to the vital energies necessary for nondepletion of the instrument and the contact level. Did that mean that we should look at the instrument's vital energies or be careful of our own vital energies?

RA: I am Ra. Each entity is responsible for itself. The mechanics of this process taking place involve firstly, the use of the physical bodily complex of third density with its accompanying physical material in order to voice these words. Thus this instrument needs to watch its vital energies carefully, for we do not wish to deplete this instrument. Secondly, the function of the supporting group may be seen to be firstly, that of protection for this contact; secondly, that of energizing the instrument and intensifying its vital energies.

This supporting group has always, due to an underlying harmony, been of a very stable nature as regards protection in love and light, thus ensuring the continuation of this narrow band contact. However, the vital energies of either of the supporting members being depleted, the instrument must then use a larger portion of its vital energies, thus depleting itself more than would be profitable on a long-term basis.

Please understand that we ask your apology for this infringement upon your free will. However, it is our distortion/understanding that you would prefer this information rather than, being left totally to your own dedication/distortion, deplete the instrument or deplete the group to the point where the contact cannot be sustained.

QUESTIONER: Can you give us advice on how to maintain the best possible condition for maintaining contact?

RA: I am Ra. We have given information concerning the proper nurturing of this channel. We, therefore, repeat ourselves only in two ways in general. Firstly, we suggest that rather than being, shall we say, brave and ignoring a physical complex weakness/distortion it is good to share this distortion with the group and thus perhaps, shall we say, remove one opportunity for contact which is very wearying for the instrument, in order that another opportunity might come about in which the instrument is properly supported.

Secondly, the work begun in harmony may continue in harmony, thanksgiving and praise of opportunities and of the Creator. These are your protections. These are our suggestions. We cannot be specific for your free will is of the essence in this contact. As we said, we only speak to this subject because of our grasp of your orientation towards long-term maintenance of this contact. This is acceptable to us.

QUESTIONER: Thank you very much. We have a device for so-called color therapy, and since we were on the concept of the different colors in the last session I was wondering if this would in some way apply to the principle of color therapy in the shining of particular colors on the physical body. Does this create a beneficial effect and can you tell me something about it?

RA: I am Ra. This therapy, as you call it, is a somewhat clumsy and variably useful tool for instigating in an entity's mind/body/spirit complex an intensification of energies or vibrations which may be of aid to the entity. The variableness of this device is due firstly to the lack of true colors used, secondly, to the extreme variation in sensitivity to vibration among your peoples.

QUESTIONER: I would think that you could achieve a true color by passing light through a crystal of the particular color. Is this correct?

RA: I am Ra. This would be one way of approaching accuracy in color. It is a matter of what you would call quality control that the celluloid used is of a varying color. This is not of a great or even visible variation, however, it does make some difference given specific applications.

QUESTIONER: Possibly you could use a prism breaking white light into its spectrum and screening off all parts of the spectrum except that which you wish to use by passing it through a slit. Would this be true?

RA: I am Ra. This is correct.

QUESTIONER: I was wondering if there is a programming of experiences that causes an individual to get certain catalysts in his daily life. For instance, as we go through our daily life there are many things which we can experience. We can look at these experiences as occurring by pure chance or by a conscious design of our own such as making appointments or going places. I was wondering if there was a behind-the-scenes, as you might call it, programming of catalyst to create the necessary experiences for more rapid growth in the case of some entities. Does this happen?

RA: I am Ra. We believe we grasp the heart of your query. Please request further information if we are not correct.

The incarnating entity which has become conscious of the incarnative process and thus programs its own experience may choose the amount of catalyst or, to phrase this differently, the number of lessons which it will undertake to experience and to learn from in one incarnation. This does not mean that all is predestined, but rather that there are invisible guidelines shaping events which will function according to this programming. Thus if one opportunity is missed another will appear until the, shall we say, student of the life experience grasps that a lesson is being offered and undertakes to learn it.

QUESTIONER: Then these lessons would be reprogrammed, you might say, as the life experience continues. Let's say that an entity develops the bias that he actually didn't choose to develop prior to incarnation. It is then possible to program experiences so that he will have an opportunity to alleviate this bias through balancing. Is this correct?

RA: I am Ra. This is precisely correct.

QUESTIONER: Thank you. From this I would extrapolate to the conjecture that the orientation in mind of the entity is the only thing that is of any consequence at all. The physical catalyst that he experiences, regardless of what is happening about him, will be a function strictly of his orientation in mind. I will use as an example (example deleted) this being a statement of the orientation in mind governing the catalyst. Is this correct?

RA: I am Ra. We prefer not to use any well-known examples, sayings, or adages in our communications to you due to the tremendous amount of distortion which any well-known saying has undergone. Therefore, we may answer the first part of your query asking that you delete the example. It is completely true to the best of our knowledge that the orientation or polarization of the mind/body/spirit complex is the cause of the perceptions generated by each entity. Thus a scene may be observed in your grocery store. The entity ahead of self may be without sufficient funds. One entity may then take this opportunity to steal. Another may take this opportunity to feel itself a failure. Another may unconcernedly remove the least necessary items, pay for what it can, and go about its business. The one behind the self, observing, may feel compassion, may feel an insult because of standing next to a poverty-stricken person, may feel generosity, may feel indifference.

Do you now see the analogies in a more appropriate manner?

QUESTIONER: I think that I do. Then from this I will extrapolate the concept which is somewhat more difficult because as you have explained before, even fourth-density positive has the concept of defensive action, but above the level of fourth density the concept of defensive action is not in use. The concept of defensive action and offensive action are very much in use in our present density.

I am assuming that if an entity is polarized strongly enough in his thought in a positive sense that defensive action is not going to be necessary for him because the opportunity to apply defensive action will never originate for him. Is this correct?

RA: I am Ra. This is unknowable. In each case, as we have said, an entity able to program experiences may choose the number and the intensity of lessons to be learned. It is possible that an extremely positively oriented entity might program for itself situations testing the ability of self to refrain from defensive action even to the point of the physical death of self or other-self. This is an intensive lesson and it is not known, shall we say, what entities have programmed. We may, if we desire, read this programming. However, this is an infringement and we choose not to do so.

QUESTIONER: I will ask you if you are familiar with a motion picture called *The Ninth Configuration*. Are you familiar with this?

RA: I am Ra. We scan your mind and see this configuration called *The Ninth Configuration*.

QUESTIONER: This motion picture brought out the point about which we have been talking. The Colonel had to make a decision. I was wondering about his polarization. He could have knuckled under, you might say, to the negative forces, but he chose to defend his friend instead. Is it possible for you to estimate which is more positively polarizing: to defend the positively oriented entity, or to allow suppression by the negatively oriented entities?

RA: I am Ra. This question takes in the scope of fourth density as well as your own and its answer may best be seen by the action of the entity called Jehoshuah, which you call Jesus. This entity was to be defended by its friends. The entity reminded its friends to put away the sword. This entity then delivered itself to be put to the physical death. The impulse to protect the loved other-self is one which persists through the fourth density, a density abounding in compassion. More than this we cannot and need not say.

QUESTIONER: Thank you. As we near the end of this master cycle there may be an increasing amount of catalyst for entities. I am wondering if, as the planetary vibrations mismatch somewhat with the fourth-density vibrations and catalyst is increased, if this will create more polarization thereby getting a slightly greater harvest?

RA: I am Ra. The question must be answered in two parts. Firstly, the planetary catastrophes, as you may call them, are a symptom of the difficult harvest rather than a consciously programmed catalyst for harvest. Thus we do not concern ourselves with it, for it is random in respect to conscious catalyst such as we may make available.

The second portion is this: the results of the random catalyst of what you call the Earth changes are also random. Thus we may see probability/possibility vortices going towards positive and negative. However, it will be as it will be. The true opportunities for conscious catalyst are not a function of the Earth changes but of the result of the seniority system of incarnations which at the time of the harvest has placed in incarnation those whose chances of using life experiences to become harvestable are the best.

QUESTIONER: Is this seniority system also used in the service-to-self side for becoming harvestable on that side?

RA: I am Ra. This is correct. You may ask one more full question at this time.

QUESTIONER: What I would like for you to do is list all the major mechanisms designed to provide catalytic experience that do not include interaction with other-self. That is the first part.

RA: I am Ra. We grasp from this question that you realize that the primary mechanism for catalytic experience in third density is other-self. The list of other catalytic influences: firstly, the Creator's universe; secondly, the self.

QUESTIONER: Can you list any sub-headings under self or ways the self is acted upon catalytically which would produce experience?

RA: I am Ra. Firstly, the self unmanifested. Secondly, the self in relation to the societal self created by self and other-self. Thirdly, the interaction between self and the gadgets, toys, and amusements of the self, other-self invention. Fourthly, the self-relationship with those attributes which you may call war and rumors of war.

QUESTIONER: I was thinking possibly of the catalyst of physical pain. Does this go under this heading?

RA: I am Ra. This is correct, it going under the heading of the unmanifested self; that is, the self which does not need other-self in order to manifest or act.

QUESTIONER: Do we have enough time left to ask the second part of this question which is to list all major mechanisms designed to provide the catalyst that include action with other-self?

RA: I am Ra. You have much time for this, for we may express this list in one of two ways. We could speak infinitely, or we could simply state that any interaction betwixt self and other-self has whatever potential for catalyst that there exists in the potential difference between self and other-self, this moderated and undergirded by the constant fact of the Creator as self and as other-self. You may ask to this question further if you wish specific information.

QUESTIONER: I believe that this is sufficient for the time being.

RA: I am Ra. Do you have a brief query or two before we close this working?

QUESTIONER: Yes, here is one question. Is there any difference in violet-ray activity or brightness between entities who are at entrance level both positive and negative to fourth density?

RA: I am Ra. This correct. The violet ray of the positive fourth density will be tinged with the green, blue, indigo triad of energies. This tinge may be seen as a portion of a rainbow or prism, as you know it, the rays being quite distinct.
  The violet ray of fourth-density negative has in its aura, shall we say, the tinge of red, orange, yellow, these rays being muddied rather than distinct.

QUESTIONER: What would the rays of fifth and sixth density look like?

RA: I am Ra. We may speak only approximately. However, we hope you understand, shall we say, that there is a distinctive difference in the color structure of each density.

Fifth density is perhaps best described as extremely white in vibration.

The sixth density of a whiteness which contains a golden quality as you would perceive it; these colors having to do with the blending into wisdom of the compassion learned in fourth density, then in sixth the blending of wisdom back into an unified understanding of compassion viewed with wisdom. This golden color is not of your spectrum but is what you would call alive.

You may ask one more question briefly.

QUESTIONER: Then I will ask if there is anything that we can do to make the instrument more comfortable or to improve the contact?

RA: I am Ra. This working is well. You are attempting to be conscientious. We thank you. May we say we enjoyed your vision of our social memory complex drinking one of your liquids while speaking through this instrument.

I am Ra. I leave you in the love and in the light of the One Infinite Creator. Go forth, then, rejoicing in the power and the peace of the One Infinite Creator. Adonai.

Session 34,
March 4, 1981

RA: I am Ra. I greet you in the love and in the light of the One Infinite Creator. We communicate now.

QUESTIONER: You stated at an earlier time that penetration of the eighth level or intelligent infinity allows a mind/body/spirit complex to be harvested if it wishes at any time/space during the cycle. When this penetration of the eighth level occurs what does the entity who penetrates it experience?

RA: I am Ra. The experience of each entity is unique in its perception of intelligent infinity. Perceptions range from a limitless joy to a strong dedication to service to others while in the incarnated state. The entity which reaches intelligent infinity most often will perceive this experience as one of unspeakable profundity. However, it is not usual for the entity to immediately desire the cessation of the incarnation. Rather the desire to communicate or use this experience to aid others is extremely strong.

QUESTIONER: Thank you. Would you define karma?

RA: I am Ra. Our understanding of karma is that which may be called inertia. Those actions which are put into motion will continue using the ways of balancing until such time as the controlling or higher principle which you may liken unto your braking or stopping is invoked. This stoppage of the inertia of action may be called forgiveness. These two concepts are inseparable.

QUESTIONER: If an entity develops what is called karma in an incarnation, is there then programming that sometimes occurs so that he will experience catalysts that will enable him to get to a point of forgiveness thereby alleviating the karma?

RA: I am Ra. This is, in general, correct. However, both self and any involved other-self may, at any time through the process of understanding, acceptance, and forgiveness, ameliorate these patterns. This is true at any point in an incarnative pattern. Thus one who has set in motion an action may forgive itself and never again make that error. This also brakes or stops what you call karma.

QUESTIONER: Thank you. Can you give me examples of catalytic action from the last session beginning with the self unmanifested producing learning catalyst?

RA: I am Ra. We observed your interest in the catalyst of pain. This experience is most common among your entities. The pain may be of the physical complex. More often it is of the mental and emotional complex. In some few cases the pain is spiritual in complex nature. This creates a potential for learning. The lessons to be learned vary. Almost always these lessons include patience, tolerance, and the ability for the light touch.

Very often the catalyst for emotional pain, whether it be the death of the physical complex of one other-self which is loved or other seeming loss, will simply result in the opposite, in a bitterness and impatience, a souring. This is catalyst which has gone awry. In these cases then there will be additional catalyst provided to offer the unmanifested self further opportunities for discovering the self as all-sufficient Creator containing all that there is and full of joy.

QUESTIONER: Do what we call contagious diseases play any part in this process with respect to the unmanifested self?

RA: I am Ra. These so-called contagious diseases are those entities of second density which offer an opportunity for this type of catalyst. If this catalyst is unneeded, then these second-density creatures, as you would call them, do not have an effect. In each of these generalizations you may please note that there are anomalies so that we cannot speak to every circumstance but only to the general run or way of things as you experience them.

QUESTIONER: What part do what we call birth defects play in this process?

RA: I am Ra. This is a portion of the programming of the mind/body/spirit complex totality manifested in the mind/body/spirit of third density. These defects are planned as limitations which are part of the experience intended by the entity's totality complex. This includes genetic predispositions, as you may call them.

QUESTIONER: Thank you. Can you give me the same type of information about the self in relation to the societal self?

RA: I am Ra. The unmanifested self may find its lessons those which develop any of the energy influx centers of the mind/body/spirit complex. The societal and self interactions most often concentrate upon the second and third energy centers. Thus those most active in attempting to remake or alter the society are those working from feelings of being correct personally or of having answers which will put power in a more correct configuration. This may be seen to be of a full travel from negative to positive in orientation. Either will activate these energy ray centers.

There are some few whose desires to aid society are of a green-ray nature or above. These entities, however, are few due to the understanding, may we say, of fourth ray that universal love freely given is more to be desired than principalities or even the rearrangement of peoples or political structures.

QUESTIONER: If an entity were to be strongly biased toward positive societal effects, what would this do to his yellow ray in the aura as opposed to an entity who wanted to create an empire of society and govern it with an iron fist?

RA: I am Ra. Let us take two such positively oriented active souls no longer in your physical time/space. The one known as Albert went into a strange and, to it, a barbaric society in order that it might heal.

This entity was able to mobilize great amounts of energy and what you call money. This entity spent much green-ray energy both as a healer and as a lover of your instrument known as the organ. This entity's yellow ray was bright and crystallized by the efforts needed to procure the funds to promulgate its efforts. However, the green and blue rays were of a toweringly brilliant nature as well. The higher levels, as you may call them, being activated, the lower, as you may call them, energy points remaining in a balance, being quite, quite bright.

The other example is the entity, Martin. This entity dealt in a great degree with rather negative orange-ray and yellow-ray vibratory patterns. However, this entity was able to keep open the green-ray energy and due to the severity of its testing, if anything, this entity may be seen to have polarized more towards the positive due to its fidelity to service to others in the face of great catalyst.

QUESTIONER: Could you give me the last names of Albert and Martin?

RA: I am Ra. These entities are known to you as Albert Schweitzer and Martin Luther King.

QUESTIONER: I thought that that was correct, but I wasn't sure. Can you give me the same type of information that we have been getting here with respect to the unmanifested interacting between self and gadgets and toys and inventions?

RA: I am Ra. In this particular instance we again concentrate for the most part in the orange and in the yellow energy centers. In a negative sense many of the gadgets among your peoples, that is what you call your communication devices and other distractions such as the less competitive games, may be seen to have the distortion of keeping the mind/body/spirit complex unactivated so that yellow- and orange-ray activity is much weakened thus carefully decreasing the possibility of eventual green-ray activation.

Others of your gadgets may be seen to be tools whereby the entity explores the capabilities of its physical or mental complexes and in some few cases, the spiritual complex, thus activating the orange ray in what you call your team sports and in other gadgets such as your modes of transport. These may be seen to be ways of investigating the feelings of power; more especially, power over others or a group power over another group of other-selves.

QUESTIONER: What is the general overall effect of television on our society with respect to this catalyst?

RA: I am Ra. Without ignoring the green-ray attempts of many to communicate via this medium such information of truth and beauty as may be helpful, we must suggest that the sum effect of this gadget is that of distraction and sleep.

QUESTIONER: Can you give me the same type of information that we are working on now with respect to war and rumors of war?

RA: I am Ra. You may see this in relationship to your gadgets. This war and self relationship is a fundamental perception of the maturing entity. There is a great chance to accelerate in whatever direction is desired. One may polarize negatively by assuming bellicose attitudes for whatever reason. One may find oneself in the situation of war and polarize somewhat towards the positive activating orange, yellow, and then green rays by heroic, if you may call them this, actions taken to preserve the mind/body/spirit complexes of other-selves.

Finally, one may polarize very strongly third ray by expressing the principle of universal love at the total expense of any distortion towards involvement in bellicose actions. In this way the entity may become a conscious being in a very brief span of your time/space. This may be seen to be what you would call a traumatic progression. It is to be noted that among your entities a large percentage of all progression has as catalyst, trauma.

QUESTIONER: You just used the term third ray in that statement. Was that the term you meant to use?

RA: I am Ra. We intended the green ray. Our difficulty lies in our perception of red ray and violet ray as fixed; thus the inner rays are those which are varying and are to be observed as those indications of seniority in the attempts to form an harvest.

QUESTIONER: Would the red ray, an intense red ray, then be used as an index for seniority in incarnation as well as an intense violet ray?

RA: I am Ra. This is partially correct. In the graduation or harvesting to fourth-density positive, the red ray is seen only as that, which being activated, is the basis for all that occurs in vibratory levels, the sum of this being violet-ray energy.

This violet ray is the only consideration for fourth-density positive. In assessing the harvestable fourth-density negative, the intensity of the red as well as the orange and the yellow rays is looked upon quite carefully as a great deal of stamina and energy of this type is necessary for the negative progression, it being extremely difficult to open the gateway to intelligent infinity from the solar plexus center. This is necessary for harvest in fourth-density negative.

QUESTIONER: Is it possible for you to use as an example our General Patton and tell me the effect that war had on him in his development?

RA: I am Ra. This will be the last full question of this working.

The one of whom you speak, known as George, was one in whom the programming of previous incarnations had created a pattern or inertia which was irresistible in its incarnation in your time/space. This entity was of a strong yellow-ray activation with frequent green-ray openings and occasional blue-ray openings. However, it did not find itself able to break the mold of previous traumatic experiences of a bellicose nature.

This entity polarized somewhat towards the positive in its incarnation due to its singleness of belief in truth and beauty. This entity was quite sensitive. It felt a great honor/duty to the preservation of that which was felt by the entity to be true, beautiful, and in need of defense. This entity perceived itself a gallant figure. It polarized somewhat towards the negative in its lack of understanding the green ray it carried with it, rejecting the forgiveness principle which is implicit in universal love.

The sum total of this incarnation vibrationally was a slight increase in positive polarity but a decrease in harvestability due to the rejection of the Law or Way of Responsibility; that is, seeing universal love, yet still it fought on.

QUESTIONER: Do we have enough time for me to ask if the death, almost immediately after the cessation of war, of this entity could have been so that it could have immediately been reincarnated so that it could make harvest?

RA: I am Ra. This is precisely correct.

QUESTIONER: Thank you. Then I will just ask if there is anything that we can do to make the instrument more comfortable or to improve the contact?

RA: I am Ra. All is well. We leave you, my friends, in the love and the light of the One which is All in All. I leave you in an ever-lasting peace. Go forth, therefore, rejoicing in the power and the peace of the One Infinite Creator. Adonai.

Session 35,
March 6, 1981

RA: I am Ra. I greet you in the love and in the light of the One Infinite Creator. We communicate now.

QUESTIONER: I would like to say that we consider it a great privilege to be doing this work, and we hope that we will be questioning in the direction that will be of value to the readers of this material. I thought that in this session it might be helpful to inspect the effect of the rays of different well-known figures in history to aid in understanding how the catalyst of the illusion creates spiritual growth. I was making a list that I thought we might use to hit the high points on the workings of the catalysts on these individuals starting with the one we know as Franklin D. Roosevelt. Could you say something about that entity?

RA: I am Ra. It is to be noted that in discussing those who are well known among your peoples there is the possibility that information may be seen to be specific to one entity whereas in actuality the great design of experience is much the same for each entity. It is with this in mind that we would discuss the experiential forces which offered catalyst to an individual.

It is further to be noted that in the case of those entities lately incarnate much distortion may have taken place in regard to misinformation and misinterpretation of an entity's thoughts or behaviors.

We shall now proceed to, shall we say, speak of the basic parameters of the one known as Franklin. When any entity comes into third-density incarnation, each of its energy centers is potentiated but must be activated by the self using experience.

The one known as Franklin developed very quickly up through red, orange, yellow, and green and began to work in the blue-ray energy center at a tender age, as you would say. This rapid growth was due, firstly, to previous achievements in the activation of the rays, secondly, to the relative comfort and leisure of its early existence, thirdly, due to the strong desire upon the part of the entity to progress. This entity mated with an entity whose blue ray vibrations were of a strength more than equal to its own thus acquiring catalyst for further growth in that area that was to persist throughout the incarnation.

This entity had some difficulty with continued green-ray activity due to the excessive energy which was put into the activities regarding other-selves in the distortion towards acquiring power. This was to have its toll upon the physical vehicle, as you may call it. The limitation of the nonmovement of a portion of the physical vehicle opened once again, for this entity, the opportunity for concentration upon the more, shall we say, universal or idealistic aspects of power; that is, the nonabusive use of power. Thus at the outset of a bellicose action this entity had lost some positive polarity due to excessive use of the orange- and yellow-ray energies at the expense of green- and blue-ray energies, then had regained the polarity due to the catalytic effects of a painful limitation upon the physical complex.

This entity was not of a bellicose nature but rather during the conflict continued to vibrate in green ray working with the blue-ray energies. The entity who was the one known as Franklin's teacher also functioned greatly during this period as blue-ray activator, not only for its mate but also in a more universal expression. This entity polarized continuously in a positive fashion in the universal sense while, in a less universal sense, developing a pattern of what may be called karma; this karma having to do with inharmonious relationship distortions with the mate/teacher.

QUESTIONER: Two things I would like to clear up. First, then Franklin's teacher was his wife? Is this correct?

RA: I am Ra. This is correct.

QUESTIONER: Secondly, did Franklin place the physical limitation on his body himself?

RA: I am Ra. This is partially correct. The basic guidelines for the lessons and purposes of incarnation had been carefully set forth before incarnation by the mind/body/spirit complex totality. If the one known as Franklin had avoided the excessive enjoyment of or attachment to the competitiveness which may be seen to be inherent in the processes of its occupation, this entity would not have had the limitation.

However, the desire to serve and to grow was strong in this programming and when the opportunities began to cease due to these distortions towards love of power the entity's limiting factor was activated.

QUESTIONER: I would now like to ask for the same type of information with respect to Adolf Hitler. You have given a little of this already. It is not necessary for you to recover what you have already given. Could you complete that information?

RA: I am Ra. In speaking of the one you call Adolf we have some difficulty due to the intense amount of confusion present in this entity's life patterns as well as the great confusion which greets any discussion of this entity.

Here we see an example of one who, in attempting activation of the highest rays of energy while lacking the green-ray key, canceled itself out as far as polarization either towards positive or negative. This entity was basically negative. However, its confusion was such that the personality disintegrated, thus leaving the mind/body/spirit complex unharvestable and much in need of healing.

This entity followed the pattern of negative polarization which suggests the elite and the enslaved, this being seen by the entity to be of an helpful nature for the societal structure. However, in drifting from the conscious polarization into what you may call a twilight world where dream took the place of events in your space/time continuum, this entity failed in its attempt to serve the Creator in an harvestable degree along the path of service to self. Thus we see the so-called insanity which may often arise when an entity attempts to polarize more quickly than experience may be integrated.

We have advised and suggested caution and patience in previous communications and do so again, using this entity as an example of the over-hasty opening of polarization without due attention to the synthesized and integrated mind/body/spirit complex. To know your self is to have the foundation upon firm ground.

QUESTIONER: Thank you. That is an important example I believe. I was wondering if any of those who were subordinate to Adolf at that time were able to polarize in a harvestable nature on the negative path?

RA: I am Ra. We can speak only of two entities who may be harvestable in a negative sense, others still being in the physical incarnation: one known to you as Hermann; the other known, as it preferred to be called, Himmler.

QUESTIONER: Thank you. Earlier we discussed Abraham Lincoln as a rather unique case. Is it possible for you to tell us why the fourth-density being used Abraham Lincoln's body, what its orientation was, and when this took place with respect to the activities that were occurring in our society at that time?

RA: I am Ra. This is possible.

QUESTIONER: Would it be of value for the reader to know this in your estimation?

RA: I am Ra. You must shape your queries according to your discernment.

QUESTIONER: Well in that case I would like to know the motivation for this use of Abraham Lincoln's body at that time?

RA: I am Ra. This shall be the last full query of this session as we find the instrument quite low in vital energies.

The one known as Abraham had an extreme difficulty in many ways and, due to physical, mental, and spiritual pain, was weary of life but without the orientation to self-destruction. In your time, 1853, this entity was contacted in sleep by a fourth-density being. This being was concerned with the battles between the forces of light and the forces of darkness which have been waged in fourth density for many of your years.

This entity accepted the honor/duty of completing the one known as Abraham's karmic patterns and the one known as Abraham discovered that this entity would attempt those things which the one known as Abraham desired to do but felt it could not. Thus the exchange was made.

The entity, Abraham, was taken to a plane of suspension until the cessation of its physical vehicle much as though we of Ra would arrange with this instrument to remain in the vehicle, come out of the trance state, and function as this instrument, leaving this instrument's mind and spirit complex in its suspended state.

The planetary energies at this time were at what seemed to this entity to be at a critical point, for that which you know as freedom had gained in acceptance as a possibility among many peoples. This entity saw the work done by those beginning the democratic concept of freedom, as you call it, in danger of being abridged or abrogated by the rising belief and use of the principle of the enslavement of entities. This is a negative concept of a fairly serious nature in your density. This entity, therefore, went forward into what it saw as the battle for the light, for healing of a rupture in the concept of freedom.

This entity did not gain or lose karma by these activities due to its detachment from any outcome. Its attitude throughout was one of service to others, more especially to the downtrodden or enslaved. The polarity of the individual was somewhat, but not severely, lessened by the cumulative feelings and thought-forms which were created due to large numbers of entities leaving the physical plane due to trauma of battle.

May we ask if this is the information you requested or if we may supply any further information?

QUESTIONER: I will ask any further questions during the next working period which should occur in about four days. We do not want to overtire the instrument. I will only ask if there is anything that we can do to make the instrument more comfortable or to improve the contact?

RA: I am Ra. All is well. I leave you, my friends, in the love and the light of the One Infinite Creator. Go forth, therefore rejoicing in the power and the peace of the One Creator. Adonai.

Session 36, March 10, 1981

RA: I am Ra. I greet you in the love and the light of the One Infinite Creator. We communicate now.

QUESTIONER: In previous communications you have spoken of the mind/body/spirit complex totality. Would you please give us a definition of the mind/body/spirit complex totality?

RA: I am Ra. There is a dimension in which time does not have sway. In this dimension, the mind/body/spirit in its eternal dance of the present may be seen in totality, and before the mind/body/spirit complex which then becomes a part of the social memory complex is willingly absorbed into the allness of the One Creator, the entity knows itself in its totality.

This mind/body/spirit complex totality functions as, shall we say, a resource for what you perhaps would call the Higher Self. The Higher Self, in turn, is a resource for examining the distillations of third-density experience and programming further experience. This is also true of densities four, five, and six with the mind/body/spirit complex totality coming into consciousness in the course of seventh density.

QUESTIONER: Then would the mind/body/spirit complex totality be responsible for programming changes in catalyst during a third-density experience of the mind/body/spirit complex so that the proper catalyst would be added, shall we say, as conditions for the complex changed during third-density experience?

RA: I am Ra. This is incorrect. The Higher Self, as you call it, that is, that self which exists with full understanding of the accumulation of experiences of the entity, aids the entity in achieving healing of the experiences which have not been learned properly and assists as you have indicated in further life experience programming, as you may call it.

The mind/body/spirit complex totality is that which may be called upon by the Higher Self aspect just as the mind/body/spirit complex calls upon the Higher Self. In the one case you have a structured situation within the space/time continuum with the Higher Self having available to it the totality of experiences which have been collected by an entity and a very firm grasp of the lessons to be learned in this density.

The mind/body/spirit complex totality is as the shifting sands and is in some part a collection of parallel developments of the same entity. This information is made available to the Higher Self aspect. This aspect may then use these projected probability/possibility vortices in order to better aid in what you would call future life programming.

QUESTIONER: Out of the Seth Material we have a statement in which Seth says that each entity here on Earth is one part of or aspect of a Higher Self or Oversoul which has many aspects or parts in many dimensions all of which learn lessons which allow the Higher Self to progress in a balanced manner. Am I to understand from this that there are many experiences similar to the one which we experience in the third density which are governed by a single Higher Self?

RA: I am Ra. The correctness of this statement is variable. The more in balance an entity becomes, the less the possibility/probability vortices may need to be explored in parallel experiences.

QUESTIONER: Do I understand from this then that the Higher Self or Oversoul may break down into numerous units if the experience is required to what we would call simultaneously experience different types of catalysts and then oversee these experiences?

RA: I am Ra. This is a statement we cannot say to be correct or incorrect due to the confusions of what you call time. True simultaneity is available only when all things are seen to be occurring at once. This overshadows the concept of which you speak. The concept of various parts of the being living experiences of varying natures simultaneously is not precisely accurate due to your understanding that this would indicate that this was occurring with true simultaneity. This is not the case.

The case is from universe to universe and parallel existences can then be programmed by the Higher Self, given the information available from the mind/body/spirit complex totality regarding the probability/possibility vortices at any crux.

QUESTIONER: Could you give an example of how this programming by the Higher Self would then bring about education through parallel experiences?

RA: I am Ra. Perhaps the simplest example of this apparent simultaneity of existence of two selves, which are in truth one self at the same time/space, is this: the Oversoul, as you call it, or Higher Self, seems to exist simultaneously with the mind/body/spirit complex which it aids. This is not actually simultaneous, for the Higher Self is moving to the mind/body/spirit complex as needed from a position in development of the entity which would be considered in the future of this entity.

QUESTIONER: Then the Higher Self operates from the future as we understand things. In other words my Higher Self would operate from what I consider to be my future? Is this correct?

RA: I am Ra. From the standpoint of your space/time, this is correct.

QUESTIONER: In that case my Higher Self would have a very large advantage in knowing what was needed since it would know, as far as I am concerned, what was going to happen. Is this correct?

RA: I am Ra. This is incorrect, in that this would be an abrogation of free will. The Higher Self aspect is aware of the lessons learned through the sixth density. The progress rate is fairly well understood. The choices which must be made to achieve the Higher Self as it is are in the provenance of the mind/body/spirit complex itself.

Thus the Higher Self is like the map in which the destination is known; the roads are very well known, these roads being designed by intelligent infinity working through intelligent energy. However, the Higher Self aspect can program only for the lessons and certain pre-disposing limitations if it wishes. The remainder is completely the free choice of each entity. There is the perfect balance between the known and the unknown.

QUESTIONER: I'm sorry for having so much trouble with these concepts, but they are very difficult I am sure to translate into our understanding and language. Some of my questions may be rather ridiculous, but does this Higher Self have some type of vehicle like our physical vehicle? Does it have a bodily complex?

RA: I am Ra. This is correct. The Higher Self is of a certain advancement within sixth density going into the seventh. After the seventh has been well entered the mind/body/spirit complex becomes so totally a mind/body/spirit complex totality that it begins to gather spiritual mass and approach the octave density. Thus the looking backwards is finished at that point.

QUESTIONER: Is the Higher Self of every entity of a sixth-density nature?

RA: I am Ra. This is correct. This is an honor/duty of self to self as one approaches seventh density.

QUESTIONER: Let me be sure that I understand this then. We have spoken of certain particular individuals. For instance we were speaking of George Patton in a previous communication. Then his Higher Self at the time of his incarnation here as George Patton about forty years ago was of sixth density? Is this correct?

RA: I am Ra. This is correct. We make note at this time that each entity has several beings upon which to call for inner support. Any of these may be taken by an entity to be the mind/body/spirit complex totality. However, this is not the case. The mind/body/spirit complex totality is a nebulous collection of all that may occur held in understanding; the Higher Self itself a projection or manifestation of mind/body/spirit complex totality which then may communicate with the mind/body/spirit during the discarnate part of a cycle of rebirth or during the incarnation; may communicate if the proper pathways or channels through the roots of mind are opened.

QUESTIONER: These channels would then be opened by meditation and I am assuming that the intense polarization would help in this. Is this correct?

RA: I am Ra. This is partially correct. Intense polarization does not necessarily develop, in the mind/body/spirit complex, the will or need to contact the Oversoul. Each path of life experience is unique. However, given the polarization, the will is greatly enhanced and vice versa.

QUESTIONER: Let me take as an example the one that you said was called Himmler. We are assuming from this that his Higher Self was of the sixth density and it was stated that Himmler had selected the negative path. Would his Higher Self then dwell in a sixth-density negative type of situation? Can you expand on this concept?

RA: I am Ra. There are no negative beings which have attained the Oversoul manifestation, which is the honor/duty of the mind/body/spirit complex totality, of late sixth density as you would term it in your time measurements. These negatively oriented mind/body/spirit complexes have a difficulty which to our knowledge has never been overcome, for after fifth-density graduation wisdom is available but must be matched with an equal amount of love. This love/light is very, very difficult to achieve in unity when following the negative path and during the earlier part of the sixth density, society complexes of the negative orientation will choose to release the potential and leap into the sixth-density positive.

Therefore, the Oversoul which makes its understanding available to all who are ready for such aid is towards the positive. However, the free will of the individual is paramount, and any guidance given by the Higher Self may be seen in either the positive or negative polarity depending upon the choice of a mind/body/spirit complex.

QUESTIONER: Then using Himmler as an example, was his Higher Self at the time he was incarnate in the 1940s a sixth-density positively oriented Higher Self?

RA: I am Ra. This is correct.

QUESTIONER: Was Himmler in any way in contact with his Higher Self at that time when he was incarnate during the 1940s?

RA: I am Ra. We remind you that the negative path is one of separation. What is the first separation: the self from the self. The one known as Himmler did not choose to use its abilities of will and polarization to seek guidance from any source but its conscious drives, self-chosen in the life experience and nourished by previous biases created in other life experiences.

QUESTIONER: Well then let's say that when Himmler reaches sixth-density negative, would he realize that his Higher Self was positively oriented and for that reason make the jump from negative to positive orientation?

RA: I am Ra. This is incorrect. The sixth-density negative entity is extremely wise. It observes the spiritual entropy occurring due to the lack of ability to express the unity of sixth density. Thus, loving the Creator and realizing at some point that the Creator is not only self but other-self as self, this entity consciously chooses an instantaneous energy reorientation so that it may continue its evolution.

QUESTIONER: Then the sixth-density entity who has reached that point in positive orientation may choose to become what we call a Wanderer and move back. I am wondering if this ever occurs with a negatively oriented sixth-density entity? Do any ever move back as Wanderers?

RA: I am Ra. Once the negatively polarized entity has reached a certain point in the wisdom density it becomes extremely unlikely that it will choose to risk the forgetting, for this polarization is not selfless but selfish and with wisdom realizes the jeopardy of such "Wandering." Occasionally a sixth-density negative becomes a Wanderer in an effort to continue to polarize towards the negative. This is extremely unusual.

QUESTIONER: Then what is the mechanism that this unusual sixth-density entity would wish to gain to polarize more negatively through Wandering?

RA: I am Ra. The Wanderer has the potential of greatly accelerating the density whence it comes in its progress in evolution. This is due to the intensive life experiences and opportunities of the third density. Thusly the positively oriented Wanderer chooses to hazard the danger of the forgetting in order to be of service to others by radiating love of others. If the forgetting is penetrated the amount of catalyst in third density will polarize the Wanderer with much greater efficiency than shall be expected in the higher and more harmonious densities.

Similarly, the negatively oriented Wanderer dares to hazard the forgetting in order that it might accelerate its progress in evolution in its own density by serving itself in third density by offering to other-selves the opportunity to hear the information having to do with negative polarization.

QUESTIONER: Are there any examples of sixth-density negatively polarized Wanderers in our historical past?

RA: I am Ra. This information could be harmful. We withhold it. Please attempt to view the entities about you as part of the Creator. We can explain no further.

QUESTIONER: It is very difficult at times for us to get more than a small percentage of understanding of some of these concepts because of our limitation of awareness, but I think that some meditation on the information from today will help us in formulating some questions about these concepts.

RA: I am Ra. May we ask for any brief queries before we leave this instrument?

QUESTIONER: I'll just ask one short one before we close. Can you tell me what percentage of the Wanderers on Earth today have been successful in penetrating the memory block and have become aware of who they are, and finally, is there anything that we can do to make the instrument more comfortable or to improve the contact?

RA: I am Ra. We can approximate the percentage of those penetrating intelligently their status. This is between eight and one-half and nine and three-quarters percent. There is a larger percentile group of those who have a fairly well defined, shall we say, symptomology indicating to them that they are not of this, shall we say, "insanity." This amounts to a bit over fifty percent of the remainder. Nearly one-third of the remainder are aware that something about them is different, so you see there are many gradations of awakening to the knowledge of being a Wanderer. We may add that it is to the middle and first of these groups that this information will, shall we say, make sense.

This instrument is well. The resting place is somewhat deleterious in its effect upon the comfort of the dorsal side of this instrument's physical vehicle. We have mentioned this before.

You are conscientious. We leave you now, my friends.

I am Ra. I leave you in the love and in the light of the Infinite Creator. Go forth, then, rejoicing merrily in the power and the peace of the One Creator. Adonai.

Session 37,
March 12, 1981

RA: I am Ra. I greet you in the love and in the light of the One Infinite Creator. We communicate now.

QUESTIONER: You said that each third-density entity has an Higher Self in the sixth density which is moving to the mind/body/spirit complex of the entity as needed. Does this Higher Self also evolve in growth through the densities beginning with the first density, and does each Higher Self have a corresponding Higher Self advanced in densities beyond it?

RA: I am Ra. To simplify this concept is our intent. The Higher Self is a manifestation given to the late sixth-density mind/body/spirit complex as a gift from its future selfness. The mid-seventh density's last action before turning towards the allness of the Creator and gaining spiritual mass is to give this resource to the sixth-density self, moving as you measure time in the stream of time.

This self, the mind/body/spirit complex of late sixth density, has then the honor/duty of using both the experiences of its total living bank of memory of experience, thoughts, and actions, and using the resource of the mind/body/spirit complex totality left behind as a type of infinitely complex thought-form.

In this way you may see your self, your Higher Self or Oversoul, and your mind/body/spirit complex totality as three points in a circle. The only distinction is that of your time/space continuum. All are the same being.

QUESTIONER: Does each entity have an individual mind/body/spirit complex totality or do a number of entities share the same mind/body/spirit complex totality?

RA: I am Ra. Both of these statements are correct given the appropriate time/space conditions. Each entity has its totality and at the point at which a planetary entity becomes a social memory complex the totality of this union of entities also has its Oversoul and its social memory complex totality as resource. As always, the sum, spiritually speaking, is greater than the sum of its parts so that the Oversoul of a social memory complex is not the sum of the Oversouls of its member entities but operates upon the way of what we have called squares and what we grasp you prefer to call doubling.

QUESTIONER: Thank you. And thank you for that explanation of the mathematics too. Could you define spiritual mass?

RA: I am Ra. This will be the last full question of this session.

Spiritual mass is that which begins to attract the out-moving and ongoing vibratory oscillations of beingness into the gravity, speaking in a spiritual sense, well of the great central sun, core, or Creator of the infinite universes.

QUESTIONER: Since we don't want to tire the instrument I will just ask if there is anything that we can do to make the instrument more comfortable or to improve the contact?

RA: I am Ra. All is well. We leave you now in the love and the light of the One Infinite Creator. Go forth, then, rejoicing in the power and the peace of the One Infinite Creator. Adonai.

Session 38,
March 13, 1981

RA: I am Ra. I greet you in the love and in the light of the One Infinite Creator. We communicate now.

QUESTIONER: Backtracking just a little bit today I would like to know if the reason nuclear energy was brought into this density forty or so years ago had anything to do with giving the entities who were here who had caused the destruction of Maldek another chance to use nuclear energy peacefully rather than destructively?

RA: I am Ra. This is incorrect in that it places cart before horse, as your people say. The desire for this type of information attracted this data to your people. It was not given for a reason from outside influences; rather it was desired by your peoples. From this point forward your reasoning is correct in that entities had desired the second chance which you mentioned.

QUESTIONER: What was the mechanism for fulfilling the desire for the information regarding nuclear energy?

RA: I am Ra. As we understand your query the mechanism was what you may call inspiration.

QUESTIONER: Would this inspiration be an entity impressing the person desiring the information with thoughts? Would this be the mechanism of inspiration?

RA: I am Ra. The mechanism of inspiration involves an extraordinary faculty of desire or will to know or to receive in a certain area accompanied by the ability to open to and trust in what you may call intuition.

QUESTIONER: Could you tell me how each of the rays, red through violet, would appear in a perfectly balanced and undistorted entity?

RA: I am Ra. We cannot tell you this for each balance is perfect and each unique. We do not mean to be obscure.

Let us offer an example. In a particular entity, let us use as an example a Wanderer; the rays may be viewed as extremely even, red, orange, yellow. The green ray is extremely bright. This is, shall we say, balanced by a dimmer indigo. Between these two the point of balance resides, the blue ray of the communicator sparkling in strength above the ordinary. In the violet ray we see this unique spectrograph, if you will, and at the same time the pure violet surrounding the whole; this in turn, surrounded by that which mixes the red and violet ray, indicating the integration of mind, body, and spirit; this surrounded in turn by the vibratory pattern of this entity's true density.

This description may be seen to be both unbalanced and in perfect balance. The latter understanding is extremely helpful in dealing with other-selves. The ability to feel blockages is useful only to the healer. There is not properly a tiny fraction of judgment when viewing a balance in colors. Of course when we see many of the energy plexi weakened and blocked, we may understand that an entity has not yet grasped the baton and begun the race. However, the potentials are always there. All the rays fully balanced are there in waiting to be activated.

Perhaps another way to address your query is this: In the fully potentiated entity the rays mount one upon the other with equal vibratory brilliance and scintillating sheen until the surrounding color is white. This is what you may call potentiated balance in third density.

QUESTIONER: Is it possible for a third-density planet to form a social memory complex which operates in third density?

RA: I am Ra. It is possible only in the latter or seventh portion of such a density when entities are harmoniously readying for graduation.

QUESTIONER: Could you give me an example of a planet of this nature, both a third-density service-to-others type and a third-density service-to-self type at this level of attainment?

RA: I am Ra. As far as we are aware there are no negatively oriented third-density social memory complexes. Positively oriented social memory complexes of third density are not unheard of but quite rare. However, an entity from the star Sirius's planetary body has approached this planetary body twice. This entity is late third density and is part of a third-density social memory complex. This has been referred to in the previous material. The social memory complex is properly a fourth-density phenomenon.

QUESTIONER: I was wondering if that particular social memory complex from the Sirius star evolved from trees?

RA: I am Ra. This approaches correctness. Those second-density vegetation forms which graduated into third density upon this planet bearing the name of Dog were close to the tree as you know it.

QUESTIONER: I was also wondering, since action of a bellicose nature is impossible as far as I understand vegetation, would they not have the advantage as they move into third density from second to not carry a racial memory of a bellicose nature and therefore develop a more harmonious society and accelerate their evolution in this nature?

RA: I am Ra. This is correct. However, to become balanced and begin to polarize properly it is then necessary to investigate movements of all kinds, especially bellicosity.

QUESTIONER: I am assuming, then, that their investigations of bellicosity were primarily of the type that they extracted from Hixson's memory rather than warfare among themselves?

RA: I am Ra. This is correct. Entities of this heritage would find it nearly impossible to fight. Indeed, their studies of movements of all kinds is their form of meditation due to the fact that their activity is upon the level of what you would call meditation and thus must be balanced, just as your entities need constant moments of meditation to balance your activities.

QUESTIONER: I believe that this is an important point for us in understanding the balancing aspect of meditation since we have here its antithesis in another type of evolution. These entities moved, we are told by Charlie Hixson, without moving their legs. I am assuming that they used a principle that is somewhat similar to the principle of movement of your crystal bells in the movement of their physical vehicles. Is this correct?

RA: I am Ra. This is partially incorrect.

QUESTIONER: I am assuming that their method of movement is not a function of mechanical leverage such as ours, but a direct function of the mind somehow connected with the magnetic action of a planet. Is this right?

RA: I am Ra. This is largely correct. It is an electromagnetic phenomenon which is controlled by thought impulses of a weak electrical nature.

QUESTIONER: Would their craft have been visible to anyone on our planet in that area at that time? Is it of a third-density material like this chair?

RA: I am Ra. This is correct. Please ask one more full question before we close as this instrument has low vital energy at this space/time.

QUESTIONER: Could you give me some idea of what conditions are like on a fourth-density negative or service-to-self planet?

RA: I am Ra. The graduation into fourth-density negative is achieved by those beings who have consciously contacted intelligent infinity through the use of red, orange, and yellow rays of energy. Therefore, the planetary conditions of fourth-density negative include the constant alignment and realignment of entities in efforts to form dominant patterns of combined energy.

The early fourth density is one of the most intensive struggle. When the order of authority has been established and all have fought until convinced that each is in the proper placement for power structure, the social memory complex begins. Always the fourth-density effect of telepathy and the transparency of thought are attempted to be used for the sake of those at the apex of the power structure.

This, as you may see, is often quite damaging to the further polarization of fourth-density negative entities, for the further negative polarization can come about only through group effort. As the fourth-density entities manage to combine, they then polarize through such services to self as those offered by the crusaders of Orion.

You may ask more specific questions in the next session of working. Are there any brief queries before we leave this instrument?

QUESTIONER: I would just ask if there is anything that we can do to make the instrument more comfortable or to improve the contact?

RA: I am Ra. All is well. We leave you in the love and light of the One Infinite Creator. Go forth rejoicing in the power and in the peace of the one Creator. Adonai.

Session 39,
March 16, 1981

RA: I am Ra. I greet you in the love and in the light of the One Infinite Creator. We communicate now.

QUESTIONER: I noticed that most of the basic things seemed to be divided into units which total seven. In looking at a transcript by Henry Puharich of "The Nine" I found a statement by The Nine where they say, "If we get seven times the electrical equivalent of the human body then it would result in sevenon of the mass of electricity." Could you explain this?

RA: I am Ra. To explain this is beyond the abilities of your language. We shall, however, make an attempt to address this concept.

As you are aware, in the beginning of the creations set up by each Logos, there are created the complete potentials, both electrical, in the sense the one you call Larson intends, and metaphysical. This metaphysical electricity is as important in the understanding, shall we say, of this statement as is the concept of electricity.

This concept, as you are aware, deals with potentiated energy. The electron has been said to have no mass but only a field. Others claim a mass of infinitesimal measure. Both are correct. The true mass of the potentiated energy is the strength of the field. This is also true metaphysically.

However, in your present physical system of knowledge it is useful to take the mass number of the electron in order to do work that you may find solutions to other questions about the physical universe. In such a way, you may conveniently consider each density of being to have a greater and greater spiritual mass. The mass increases, shall we say, significantly but not greatly until the gateway density. In this density the summing up, the looking backwards—in short—all the useful functions of polarity have been used. Therefore, the metaphysical electrical nature of the individual grows greater and greater in spiritual mass.

For an analog one may observe the work of the one known as Albert who posits the growing to infinity of mass as this mass approaches the speed of light. Thus the seventh-density being, the completed being, the Creator who knows Itself, accumulates mass and compacts into the One Creator once again.

QUESTIONER: Then in the equation here I am assuming Mi is spiritual mass.

$$Mi = \frac{m_0 C^2}{\sqrt{1 - v^2/c^2}}$$

RA: I am Ra. This is correct.

QUESTIONER: Thank you. Can you tell me what this transmission from "The Nine" means? "CH is a principle which is the revealing principle of knowledge and of law"? Can you tell me what that principle is?

RA: I am Ra. The principle so veiled in that statement is but the simple principle of the constant or Creator and the transient or the incarnate being and the yearning existing between the two, one for the other, in love and light amidst the distortions of free will acting upon the illusion-bound entity.

QUESTIONER: Was the reason "The Nine" transmitted this principle in this form the first distortion?

RA: I am Ra. This is incorrect.

QUESTIONER: Can you tell me why they gave the principle in such a veiled form then?

RA: I am Ra. The scribe is most interested in puzzles and equations.

QUESTIONER: I see. "The Nine" describe themselves as the "nine principals of God." Can you tell me what they mean by that?

RA: I am Ra. This is also a veiled statement. The attempt is made to indicate that the nine who sit upon the Council are those representing the Creator, the One Creator, just as there may be nine witnesses in a courtroom testifying for one defendant. The term "principal" has this meaning also.

The desire of the scribe may be seen in much of this material to have affected the manner of its presentation just as the abilities and preferences of this group determine the nature of this contact. The difference lies in the fact that we are as we are. Thus we may either speak as we will or not speak at all. This demands a very tuned, shall we say, group.

QUESTIONER: I sense that there is fruitful ground for investigation of our development in tracing the evolution of the bodily energy centers because these seven centers seem to be linked with all of the sevens that I spoke of previously, and these seem to be central to our own development. Could you describe the process of evolution of these bodily energy centers starting with the most primitive form of life to have them?

RA: I am Ra. This material has been covered previously to some extent. Therefore, we shall not repeat information upon which rays dwell in first and second density and the wherefores of this, but rather attempt to enlarge upon this information.

The basic pivotal points of each level of development; that is, each density beyond second, may be seen to be as follows: Firstly, the basic energy of so-called red ray. This ray may be understood to be the basic strengthening ray for each density. It shall never be condescended to as less important or productive of spiritual evolution, for it is the foundation ray.

The next foundation ray is yellow. This is the great stepping-stone ray. At this ray the mind/body potentiates to its fullest balance. The strong red/orange/yellow triad springboards the entity into the center ray of green. This is again a basic ray but not a primary ray.

This is the resource for spiritual work. When green ray has been activated we find the third primary ray being able to begin potentiation. This is the first true spiritual ray in that all transfers are of an integrated mind/body/spirit nature. The blue ray seats the learnings/teachings of the spirit in each density within the mind/body complex animating the whole, communicating to others this entirety of beingness.

The indigo ray, though precious, is that ray worked upon only by the adept, as you would call it. It is the gateway to intelligent infinity bringing intelligent energy through. This is the energy center worked upon in those teachings considered inner, hidden, and occult, for this ray is that which is infinite in its possibilities. As you are aware, those who heal, teach, and work for the Creator in any way which may be seen to be both radiant and balanced are those activities which are indigo ray.

As you are aware, the violet ray is constant and does not figure into a discussion of the functions of ray activation in that it is the mark, the register, the identity, the true vibration of an entity.

QUESTIONER: In order to clarify a little bit I would like to ask this question: If we have a highly polarized entity polarized towards service to others and a highly polarized entity polarized towards service to self, what would be the difference in the red ray of these two entities?

RA: I am Ra. This shall be the last full question of this working.

There is no difference in equally strongly polarized positive and negative entities as regards red ray.

QUESTIONER: Is this also true of all of the other rays?

RA: I am Ra. We shall answer briefly. You may question further at another working.

The negative ray pattern is the red/orange/yellow moving directly to the blue, this only being used in order to contact intelligent infinity.

In positively oriented entities the configuration is even, crystallinely clear, and of the seven ray description.

Are there any short queries before we leave this instrument?

QUESTIONER: I would just ask if there is anything that we can do to make the instrument more comfortable and to improve the contact?

RA: I am Ra. You are most conscientious. All is well. I leave you, my friends, in the love and in the light of the One Infinite Creator. Go forth therefore rejoicing in the power and in the peace of the One Creator. Adonai.

Session 40,
March 18, 1981

RA: I am Ra. I greet you in the love and in the light of the Infinite Creator. We communicate now.

QUESTIONER: I thought that I would make a statement and let you correct it. I'm trying to make a simple model of the portion of the universe that we find ourselves in. Starting with the sub-Logos, our sun, we have white light emanating from this which is made up of the frequencies ranging from the red to the violet. I am assuming that this white light then contains the experiences through all of the densities and as we go into the eighth density we go into a black hole which becomes, on the other side, another Logos or sun and starts another octave of experience. Can you comment on this part of my statement?

RA: I am Ra. We can comment upon this statement to an extent. The concept of the white light of the sub-Logos being prismatically separated and later, at the final chapter, being absorbed again is basically correct. However, there are subtleties involved which are more than semantic.

The white light which emanates and forms the articulated sub-Logos has its beginning in what may be metaphysically seen as darkness. The light comes into that darkness and transfigures it, causing the chaos to organize and become reflective or radiant. Thus the dimensions come into being.

Conversely, the blackness of the black hole, metaphysically speaking, is a concentration of white light being systematically absorbed once again into the One Creator. Finally, this absorption into the One Creator continues until all the infinity of creations have attained sufficient spiritual mass in order that all form once again the great central sun, if you would so imagine it, of the intelligent infinity awaiting potentiation by free will. Thus the transition of the octave is a process which may be seen to enter into timelessness of unimaginable nature. To attempt to measure it by your time measures would be useless.

Therefore, the concept of moving through the black hole of the ultimate spiritual gravity well and coming immediately into the next octave misses the subconcept or corollary of the portion of this process which is timeless.

QUESTIONER: Our astronomers have noticed that light from spiral galaxies is approximately seventy times less than it should be, considering the calculated mass of the galaxy. I was wondering if that was due to the increase of spiritual mass in the galaxy in what we call white dwarf stars?

RA: I am Ra. This is basically correct and is a portion of the way or process of creation's cycle.

QUESTIONER: Thank you. I was also wondering if the first density corresponded somehow to the color red, the second to the color orange, the third to the color yellow and so on through the densities corresponding to the colors in perhaps a way so that the basic vibration which forms the photon that forms the core of all atomic particles would have a relationship to the color in the density and that that vibration would step up for second, third, and fourth density corresponding to the increase in the vibration of the colors. Is any of this correct?

RA: I am Ra. This is more correct than you have stated. Firstly, you are correct in positing a quantum, if you will, as the nature of each density and further correct in assuming that these quanta may be seen to be of vibratory natures corresponding to color as you grasp this word. However, it is also true, as you have suspected but not asked, that each density is of the metaphysical characteristic complex of its ray. Thus in first density the red ray is the foundation for all that is to come. In second density the orange ray is that of movement and growth of the individual, this ray striving towards the yellow ray of self-conscious manifestations of a social nature as well as individual; third density being the equivalent, and so forth, each density being primarily its ray plus the attractions of the following ray pulling it forward in evolution and to some extent coloring or shading the chief color of that density.

QUESTIONER: Then bodily energy centers for an individual, assuming that the individual evolves in a straight line from first through to eighth density, would then be activated to completion if everything worked as it should? Would each chakra be activated to completion and greatest intensity by the end of the experience in each density?

RA: I am Ra. Hypothetically speaking, this is correct. However, the fully activated being is rare. Much emphasis is laid upon the harmonies and balances of individuals. It is necessary for graduation across densities for the primary energy centers to be functioning in such a way as to communicate with intelligent infinity and to appreciate and bask in this light in all of its purity. However, to fully activate each energy center is the mastery of few, for each center has a variable speed of rotation or activity. The important observation to be made once all necessary centers are activated to the minimal necessary degree is the harmony and balance between these energy centers.

QUESTIONER: Thank you. Taking as an example the transition between second and third density, when this transition takes place, does the frequency of vibration which forms the photon (the core of all the particles of the density) increase from a frequency corresponding to second density or the color orange to the frequency that we measure as the color yellow? What I am getting at is, do all the vibrations that form the density, the basic vibrations of the photon, increase in a quantum fashion over a relatively short period of time?

RA: I am Ra. This is correct. Then you see within each density the gradual upgrading of vibratory levels.

QUESTIONER: This is a guess. Would the frequency going from second to third increase from the middle orange or average orange frequency to the middle or average yellow frequency?

RA: I am Ra. This query is indeterminate. We shall attempt to be of aid. However, the frequency that is the basis of each density is what may be called a true color. This term is impossible to define given your system of sensibilities and scientific measurements, for color has vibratory characteristics both in space/time and in time/space. The true color is then overlaid and tinged by the rainbow of the various vibratory levels within that density and the attraction vibrations of the next true color density.

QUESTIONER: How long was the time of transition from second to third density? A generation and a half I believe you said. Is that correct?

RA: I am Ra. This is correct, the time measured in your years being approximately 1,350.

QUESTIONER: Then what will be the time of transition on this planet from third to fourth density?

RA: I am Ra. This is difficult to estimate due to the uncharacteristic anomalies of this transition. There are at this space/time nexus beings incarnate which have begun fourth-density work. However, the third-density climate of planetary consciousness is retarding the process. At this particular nexus the possibility/probability vortices indicate somewhere between 100 and 700 of your years as transition period. This cannot be accurate due to the volatility of your peoples at this space/time.

QUESTIONER: Has the vibration of the photon increased in frequency already?

RA: I am Ra. This is correct. It is this influence which has begun to cause thoughts to become things. As an example you may observe the thoughts of anger becoming those cells of the physical bodily complex going out of control to become what you call the cancer.

QUESTIONER: I am assuming that this vibratory increase began about twenty to thirty years ago. Is this correct?

RA: I am Ra. The first harbingers of this were approximately forty-five of your years ago, the energies vibrating more intensely through the forty-year period preceding the final movement of vibratory matter, shall we say, through the quantum leap, as you would call it.

QUESTIONER: Starting then, forty-five years ago, and taking the entire increase of vibration that we will experience in this density change, approximately what percentage through this increase in vibrational change are we right now?

RA: I am Ra. The vibratory nature of your environment is true color, green. This is at this time heavily over-woven with the orange ray of planetary consciousness. However, the nature of quanta is such that the movement over the boundary is that of discrete placement of vibratory level.

QUESTIONER: You mentioned that the thoughts of anger now are causing cancer. Can you expand on this mechanism as it acts as a catalyst or its complete purpose?

RA: I am Ra. The fourth density is one of revealed information. Selves are not hidden to self or other-selves. The imbalances or distortions which are of a destructive nature show, therefore, in more obvious ways, the vehicle of the mind/body/spirit complex thus acting as a teaching resource for self-revelation. These illnesses such as cancer are correspondingly very amenable to self-healing once the mechanism of the destructive influence has been grasped by the individual.

QUESTIONER: Then you are saying that cancer is quite easily healed mentally and is a good teaching tool because it is easily healed mentally and once the entity forgives the other-self at whom he is angry, the cancer will disappear. Is this correct?

RA: I am Ra. This is partially correct. The other portion of healing has to do with forgiveness of self and a greatly heightened respect for the self. This may conveniently be expressed by taking care in dietary matters. This is quite frequently a part of the healing and forgiving process. Your basic premise is correct.

QUESTIONER: In dietary matters, what would be the foods that one would include and what would be the foods that one would exclude in a general way for the greatest care of one's bodily complex?

RA: I am Ra. Firstly, we underline and emphasize that this information is not to be understood literally but as a link or psychological nudge for the body and the mind and spirit. Thus it is the care and respect for the self that is the true thing of importance. In this light we may iterate the basic information given for this instrument's diet. The vegetables, the fruits, the grains, and to the extent necessary for the individual metabolism, the animal products. These are those substances showing respect for the self. In addition, though this has not been mentioned for this instrument is not in need of purification, those entities in need of purging the self of a poison thought-form or emotion complex do well to take care in following a program of careful fasting until the destructive thought-form has been purged analogously with the by-products of ridding the physical vehicle of excess material. Again you see the value not to the body complex but used as a link for the mind and spirit. Thus self reveals self to self.

QUESTIONER: Thank you. A very important concept. Does the fact that the basic vibration that we experience now is green true color or fourth density account for the fact that there are many mental effects upon material objects that are now observable for the first time in a mass way such as the bending of metal by mind?

RA: I am Ra. This shall be the final query in total of this working.

This is not only correct but we suggest you take this concept further and understand the great number of entities with the so-called mental diseases being due to the effect of this green-ray true color upon the mental configurations of those unready mentally to face the self for the first time.

Are there any brief queries before we close?

QUESTIONER: Just two. With respect to what you just said, would then people incarnating here by seniority of vibration who incarnate in the service-to-self path be ones who would have extreme difficulty mentally with this green-ray vibration?

RA: I am Ra. This is incorrect. It is rather the numbers who have distracted themselves and failed to prepare for this transition yet who are somewhat susceptible to its influence who may be affected.

QUESTIONER: Thank you. Is there anything that we can do to make the instrument more comfortable or to improve the contact?

RA: This instrument is well. You are conscientious. The appurtenances cause this instrument greater comfort in the distortion of the warmth of the body complex. I am Ra. I leave you, my friends, in the love and in the light of the One Infinite Creator. Go forth then rejoicing in the power and in the peace of the One Infinite Creator. Adonai.

Session 41,
March 20, 1981

RA: I am Ra. I greet you in the love and in the light of the One Infinite Creator. We communicate now.

QUESTIONER: I have one question of logistics to start with. I know that it is a dumb question, but I have to ask it to be sure. There is a possibility that we may have to move from this location. Will this have any effect at all on our contact with Ra?

RA: I am Ra. This is not a foolish question. The location is meaning-less, for are we not in the creation? However, the place of the working shall be either carefully adjudged by your selves to be of the appropriate vibratory levels or it shall be suggested that the purification of the place be enacted and dedication made through meditation before initial working. This might entail such seemingly mundane chores as the cleansing or painting of surfaces which you may deem to be inappropriately marred.

QUESTIONER: I am familiar with the Banishing Ritual of the Lesser Pentagram. I was wondering if this ritual was of use in preparing a place for this type of working?

RA: I am Ra. This is correct.

QUESTIONER: In trying to build an understanding from the start, you might say, starting with intelligent infinity and getting to our present condition of being I think that I should go back and investigate our sun since it is the sub-Logos that creates all that we experience in this particular planetary system.

Will you give me a description of our sun?

RA: I am Ra. This is a query which is not easily answered in your language, for the sun has various aspects in relation to intelligent infinity, to intelligent energy, and to each density of each planet, as you call these spheres. Moreover, these differences extend into the metaphysical or time/space part of your creation.

In relationship to intelligent infinity, the sun body is, equally with all parts of the infinite creation, part of that infinity.

In relation to the potentiated intelligent infinity which makes use of intelligent energy, it is the offspring, shall we say, of the Logos for a much larger number of sub-Logoi. The relationship is hierarchical in that the sub-Logos uses the intelligent energy in ways set forth by the Logos and uses its free will to co-create the, shall we say, full nuances of your densities as you experience them.

In relationship to the densities, the sun body may physically, as you would say, be seen to be a large body of gaseous elements undergoing the processes of fusion and radiating heat and light.

Metaphysically, the sun achieves a meaning to fourth through seventh density according to the growing abilities of entities in these densities to grasp the living creation and co-entity, or other-self, nature of this sun body. Thus by the sixth density the sun may be visited and inhabited by those dwelling in time/space and may even be partially created from moment to moment by the processes of sixth-density entities in their evolution.

QUESTIONER: In your last statement did you mean that the sixth-density entities are actually creating manifestations of the sun in their density? Could you explain what you meant by that?

RA: I am Ra. In this density some entities whose means of reproduction is fusion may choose to perform this portion of experience as part of the beingness of the sun body. Thus you may think of portions of the light that you receive as offspring of the generative expression of sixth-density love.

QUESTIONER: Then could you say that sixth-density entities are using that mechanism to be more closely co-Creators with the Infinite Creator?

RA: I am Ra. This is precisely correct as seen in the latter portions of sixth density seeking the experiences of the gateway density.

QUESTIONER: Thank you. What I want to do now is investigate, as the first density is formed, what happens and how energy centers are first formed in beings. Does it make any sense to ask you if the sun itself has a density, or is it all densities?

RA: I am Ra. The sub-Logos is of the entire octave and is not that entity which experiences the learning/teachings of entities such as yourselves.

QUESTIONER: I am going to make a statement of my understanding and ask you to correct me. I intuitively see the first-density being formed by an energy center which is a vortex. This vortex then causes these spinning motions that I have mentioned before of vibration which is light which then starts to condense into materials of the first density. Is this correct?

RA: I am Ra. This is correct as far as your reasoning has taken you. However, it is well to point out that the Logos has the plan of all the densities of the octave in potential completion before entering the space/time continuum in first density. Thus the energy centers exist before they are manifest.

QUESTIONER: Then what is the simplest being that is manifested?

I am supposing that it might be a single cell or something like that. How does it function with respect to energy centers?

RA: I am Ra. The simplest manifest being is light or what you have called the photon. In relationship to energy centers it may be seen to be the center or foundation of all articulated energy fields.

QUESTIONER: When first density is formed we have fire, air, earth, and water. There is at some time the first movement or individuation of life into a portion of consciousness that is self-mobile. Could you describe the process of the creation of this and what type of energy center it has?

RA: I am Ra. The first or red-ray density, though attracted towards growth, is not in the proper vibration for those conditions conducive to what you may call the spark of awareness. As the vibratory energies move from red to orange, the vibratory environment is such as to stimulate those chemical substances which lately had been inert to combine in such a fashion that love and light begin the function of growth.

The supposition which you had earlier made concerning single-celled entities such as the polymorphous dinoflagellate is correct. The mechanism is one of the attraction of upward spiraling light. There is nothing random about this or any portion of evolution.

QUESTIONER: As I remember, the polymorphous dinoflagellate has an iron- rather than a copper-based cell. Could you comment on that?

RA: I am Ra. This information is not central. The base of any metabolism, shall we say, is that which may be found in the chemical substances of the neighborhood of origin.

QUESTIONER: I was just commenting on this because it has the motion of our animal life with copper-based cells, yet it has the iron-based cell of plant life indicating a transition from possibly plant to animal life. Am I wrong? My memory is a little fuzzy on this.

RA: I am Ra. It is not that you are incorrect but that no conclusions should be drawn from such information. There are several different types of bases for conscious entities not only upon this planetary sphere but to a much greater extent in the forms found on planetary spheres of other sub-Logoi. The chemical vehicle is that which most conveniently houses the consciousness. The functioning of consciousness is the item of interest rather than the chemical makeup of a physical vehicle.

We have observed that those whom you call scientists have puzzled over the various differences and possible interrelationships of various stages, types, and conditions of lifeforms. This is not fruitful material as it is that which is of a moment's choice by your sub-Logos.

QUESTIONER: I didn't mean to waste time with that question but you just happened to mention that particular single cell. Does this polymorphous dinoflagellate have an orange energy center?

RA: I am Ra. This is correct.

QUESTIONER: Is this energy center, then, on a very small scale related to the orange energy center in man?

RA: I am Ra. The true color is precisely the same. However, the consciousness of the second-density beginning is primitive and the use of orange ray limited to the expression of self which may be seen to be movement and survival.

In third density, at this time, those clinging to orange ray have a much more complex system of distortions through which orange ray is manifested. This is somewhat complicated. We shall endeavor to simplify.

The appropriate true color for third density is, as you have ascertained, yellow. However, the influences of the true color, green, acting upon yellow ray entities have caused many entities to revert to the consideration of self rather than the stepping forward into consideration of other-self or green ray. This may not be seen to be of a negatively polarized nature, as the negatively polarized entity is working very intensively with the deepest manifestations of yellow-ray group energies, especially the manipulations of other-self for service to self. Those reverting to orange ray, and we may add these are many upon your plane at this time, are those who feel the vibrations of true color green and, therefore, respond by rejecting governmental and societal activities as such and seek once more the self.

However, not having developed the yellow ray properly so that it balances the personal vibratory rates of the entity, the entity then is faced with the task of further activation and balancing of the self in relation to the self, thus the orange-ray manifestations at this space/time nexus.

Thus true color orange is that which it is without difference. However, the manifestations of this or any ray may be seen to be most various depending upon the vibratory levels and balances of the mind/body or mind/body/spirit complexes which are expressing these energies.

QUESTIONER: Could you tell me the simplest and first entity to have both orange- and yellow-ray energy centers?

RA: I am Ra. Upon your planetary sphere those having the first yellow-ray experiences are those of animal and vegetable natures which find the necessity for reproduction by bisexual techniques or who find it necessary to depend in some way upon other-selves for survival and growth.

QUESTIONER: And then what entity would be the simplest that would have red, orange, yellow, and green rays activated?

RA: I am Ra. This information has been covered in a previous session. To perhaps simplify your asking, each center may be seen to be activated potentially in third density, the late second-density entities having the capability, if efficient use is made of experience, of vibrating and activating the green ray energy center.

The third-density being, having the potential for complete self-awareness, thus has the potential for the minimal activation of all energy centers. The fourth, fifth, and sixth densities are those refining the higher energy centers. The seventh density is a density of completion and the turning towards timelessness or foreverness.

QUESTIONER: Then would an animal in second density have all of the energy centers in some way in its being but just not activated?

RA: I am Ra. This is precisely correct.

QUESTIONER: Then the animal in second density is composed of light as are all things. What I am trying to get at is the relationship between the light that the various bodies of the animal are created of and the relationship of this to the energy centers which are active and the ones which are not active and how this is linked with the Logos. It is a difficult question to ask. Can you give me some kind of answer?

RA: I am Ra. The answer is to redirect your thought processes from any mechanical view of evolution. The will of the Logos posits the potentials available to the evolving entity. The will of the entity as it evolves is the single measure of the rate and fastidiousness of the activation and balancing of the various energy centers.

QUESTIONER: Thank you. In the session from the day before yesterday you mentioned variable speed of rotation or activity of energy centers. What did you mean by that?

RA: I am Ra. Each energy center has a wide range of rotational speed or as you may see it more clearly in relation to color, brilliance. The more strongly the will of the entity concentrates upon and refines or purifies each energy center, the more brilliant or rotationally active each energy center will be. It is not necessary for the energy centers to be activated in order in the case of the self-aware entity. Thusly entities may have extremely brilliant energy centers while being quite unbalanced in their violet-ray aspect due to lack of attention paid to the totality of experience of the entity.

The key to balance may then be seen in the unstudied, spontaneous, and honest response of entities toward experiences, thus using experience to the utmost, then applying the balancing exercises and achieving the proper attitude for the most purified spectrum of energy center manifestation in violet ray. This is why the brilliance or rotational speed of the energy centers is not considered above the balanced aspect or violet-ray manifestation of an entity in regarding harvestability; for those entities which are unbalanced, especially as to the primary rays, will not be capable of sustaining the impact of the love and light of intelligent infinity to the extent necessary for harvest.

QUESTIONER: Could you tell me the difference between space/time and time/space?

RA: I am Ra. Using your words, the difference is that between the visible and invisible or the physical and metaphysical. Using mathematical terms, as does the one you call Larson, the difference is that between s/t and t/s.

QUESTIONER: You mentioned in the last session the concept of fasting for removing unwanted thought-forms. Can you expand on this process and explain a little bit more about how this works?

RA: I am Ra. This, as all healing techniques, must be used by a conscious being; that is, a being conscious that the ridding of excess and unwanted material from the body complex is the analogy to the ridding of mind or spirit of excess or unwanted material. Thus the one discipline or denial of the unwanted portion as an appropriate part of the self is taken through the tree of mind down through the trunk to subconscious levels where the connection is made and thus the body, mind, and spirit, then in unison, express denial of the excess or unwanted spiritual or mental material as part of the entity.

All then falls away and the entity, while understanding, if you will, and appreciating the nature of the rejected material as part of the greater self, nevertheless, through the action of the will purifies and refines the mind/body/spirit complex, bringing into manifestation the desired mind complex or spirit complex attitude.

QUESTIONER: Then would this be like a conscious reprogramming of catalyst? For instance, for some entities catalyst is programmed by the Higher Self to create experiences so that the entity can release itself from unwanted biases. Would this be analogous then to the entity consciously programming this release and using fasting as the method of communication to itself?

RA: I am Ra. This is not only correct but may be taken further. The self, if conscious to a great enough extent of the workings of this catalyst and the techniques of programming, may through concentration of the will and the faculty of faith alone cause reprogramming without the analogy of the fasting, the diet, or other analogous body complex disciplines.

QUESTIONER: I have a book, *Initiation*, in which the woman describes initiation. Are you familiar with the contents of this book?

RA: I am Ra. This is correct. We scan your mind.

QUESTIONER: I have only read part of it, but I was wondering if the teachings in the book with respect to balancing were Ra's teachings?

RA: I am Ra. This is basically correct with distortions that may be seen when this material is collated with the material we have offered.

QUESTIONER: Why are the red, yellow, and blue energy centers called primary centers? I think from previous material I understand this, but is there some tracing of these primary colors back to intelligent infinity more profound than what you have given us?

RA: I am Ra. We cannot say what may seem profound to an entity. The red, yellow, and blue rays are primary because they signify activity of a primary nature.

Red ray is the foundation; orange ray the movement towards yellow ray which is the ray of self-awareness and interaction. Green ray is the movement through various experiences of energy exchanges having to do with compassion and all-forgiving love to the primary blue ray which is the first ray of radiation of self regardless of any actions from another.

The green-ray entity is ineffectual in the face of blockage from other-selves. The blue-ray entity is a co-Creator. This may perhaps simply be a restatement of previous activity, but if you consider the function of the Logos as representative of the Infinite Creator in effectuating the knowing of the Creator by the Creator you may perhaps see the steps by which this may be accomplished.

May we ask for one final full question before we leave this working?

QUESTIONER: This may be too long a question for this working, but I will ask it and if it is too long we can continue it at a later time. Could you tell me of the development of the social memory complex Ra, from its first beginnings and what catalysts it used to get to where it is now in activation of rays?

RA: I am Ra. The question does not demand a long answer, for we who experienced the vibratory densities upon that planetary sphere which you call Venus were fortunate in being able to move in harmony with the planetary vibrations with an harmonious graduation to second, to third, and to fourth, and a greatly accelerated fourth-density experience.

We spent much time/space, if you will, in fifth density balancing the intense compassion we had gained in fourth density. The graduation again was harmonious and our social memory complex which had become most firmly cemented in fourth density remained of a very strong and helpful nature.

Our sixth-density work was also accelerated because of the harmony of our social memory complex so that we were able to set out as members of the Confederation to even more swiftly approach graduation to seventh density. Our harmony, however, has been a grievous source of naiveté as regards working with your planet. Is there a brief query before we leave this instrument?

QUESTIONER: Is there anything that we can do to make the instrument more comfortable or to improve the contact?

RA: I am Ra. All is well. I leave you, my friends, in the love and in the light of the One Infinite Creator. Go forth, therefore, rejoicing in the power and the peace of the One Infinite Creator. Adonai.

Session 42,
March 22, 1981

RA: I am Ra. I greet you in the love and in the light of the One Infinite Creator. We communicate now.

QUESTIONER: I am going to make a statement and ask you to comment on its degree of accuracy. I am assuming that the balanced entity would not be swayed either towards positive or negative emotions by any situation which he might confront. By remaining unemotional in any situation, the balanced entity may clearly discern the appropriate and necessary responses in harmony with the Law of One for each situation. Is this correct?

RA: I am Ra. This is an incorrect application of the balancing which we have discussed. The exercise of first experiencing feelings and then consciously discovering their antitheses within the being has as its objective not the smooth flow of feelings both positive and negative while remaining unswayed but rather the objective of becoming unswayed. This is a simpler result and takes much practice, shall we say.

The catalyst of experience works in order for the learn/teachings of this density to occur. However, if there is seen in the being a response, even if it is simply observed, the entity is still using the catalyst for learn/teaching. The end result is that the catalyst is no longer needed. Thus this density is no longer needed. This is not indifference or objectivity but a finely tuned compassion and love which sees all things as love. This seeing elicits no response due to catalytic reactions. Thus the entity is now able to become co-Creator of experiential occurrences. This is the truer balance.

QUESTIONER: I will attempt to make an analogy. If an animal, shall I say, a bull, in a pen attacks you because you have wandered into his pen, you get out of his way rapidly but you do not blame him. You do not have much of an emotional response other than the response that he might damage you. However, if you encounter another self in his territory and he attacks you, your response may be more of an emotional nature creating physical bodily responses. Am I correct in assuming that when your response to the animal and to the other-self is that of seeing both as Creator and loving both and understanding their action in attacking you is the action of their free will then you have balanced yourself correctly in this area? Is this correct?

RA: I am Ra. This is basically correct. However, the balanced entity will see in the seeming attack of an other-self the causes of this action which are, in most cases, of a more complex nature than the cause of the attack of the second-density bull as was your example. Thus this balanced entity would be open to many more opportunities for service to a third-density other-self.

QUESTIONER: Would a perfectly balanced entity feel any emotional response in being attacked by the other-self?

RA: I am Ra. This is correct. The response is love.

QUESTIONER: In the illusion that we now experience it is difficult to maintain this response especially if the attack results in physical pain, but I assume that this response should be maintained even through physical pain or loss of life. Is this correct?

RA: I am Ra. This is correct and further is of a major or principle importance in understanding, shall we say, the principle of balance. Balance is not indifference but rather the observer not blinded by any feelings of separation but rather fully imbued with love.

QUESTIONER: In the last session you made the statement that "We, that is Ra, spent much time/space in the fifth density balancing the intense compassion that we had gained in the fourth density." Could you expand on this concept with respect to the material you just discussed?

RA: I am Ra. The fourth density, as we have said, abounds in compassion. This compassion is folly when seen through the eyes of wisdom. It is the salvation of third density but creates a mismatch in the ultimate balance of the entity.

Thus we, as a social memory complex of fourth density, had the tendency towards compassion even to martyrdom in aid of other-selves. When the fifth-density harvest was achieved we found that in this vibratory level flaws could be seen in the efficacy of such unrelieved compassion. We spent much time/space in contemplation of those ways of the Creator which imbue love with wisdom.

QUESTIONER: I would like to try to make an analogy for third density of this concept. Many entities here feel great compassion for relieving the physical problems of third-density other-selves by administering to them in many ways, with food if there is hunger as there is now in the African nations, by bringing them medicine if they feel that there is a need to minister to them medically, and being selfless in all of these services to a very great extent.

This is creating a vibration that is in harmony with green ray or fourth density but it is not balanced with the understanding of fifth density that these entities are experiencing catalysts and a more balanced administration to their needs would be to provide them with the learning necessary to reach the state of awareness of fourth density than it would be to minister to their physical needs at this time. Is this correct?

RA: I am Ra. This is incorrect. To a mind/body/spirit complex which is starving, the appropriate response is the feeding of the body. You may extrapolate from this.

On the other hand, however, you are correct in your assumption that the green-ray response is not as refined as that which has been imbued with wisdom. This wisdom enables the entity to appreciate its contributions to the planetary consciousness by the quality of its being without regard to activity or behavior which expects results upon visible planes.

QUESTIONER: Then why do we have the extreme starvation problem in, generally, the area of Africa at this time? Is there any metaphysical reason for this, or is it purely random?

RA: I am Ra. Your previous assumption was correct as to the catalytic action of this starvation and ill health. However, it is within the free will of an entity to respond to this plight of other-selves, and the offering of the needed foodstuffs and substances is an appropriate response within the framework of your learn/teachings at this time which involve the growing sense of love for and service to other-selves.

QUESTIONER: What is the difference in terms of energy center activation between a person who represses emotional responses to emotionally charged situations and the person who is balanced and, therefore, truly unswayed by emotionally charged situations?

RA: I am Ra. This query contains an incorrect assumption. To the truly balanced entity no situation would be emotionally charged. With this understood, we may say the following: The repression of emotions depolarizes the entity insofar as it then chooses not to use the catalytic action of the space/time present in a spontaneous manner, thus dimming the energy centers. There is, however, some polarization towards positive if the cause of this repression is consideration for other-selves. The entity which has worked long enough with the catalyst to be able to feel the catalyst but not find it necessary to express reactions is not yet balanced but suffers no depolarization due to the transparency of its experiential continuum. Thus the gradual increase in the ability to observe one's reaction and to know the self will bring the self ever closer to a true balance. Patience is requested and suggested, for the catalyst is intense upon your plane and its use must be appreciated over a period of consistent learn/teaching.

QUESTIONER: How can a person know when he is unswayed by an emotionally charged situation or if he is repressing the flow of emotions, or if he is in balance and truly unswayed?

RA: I am Ra. We have spoken to this point. Therefore, we shall briefly iterate that to the balanced entity no situation has an emotional charge but is simply a situation like any other in which the entity may or may not observe an opportunity to be of service. The closer an entity comes to this attitude the closer an entity is to balance. You may note that it is not our recommendation that reactions to catalyst be repressed or suppressed unless such reactions would be a stumbling block not consonant with the Law of One to an other-self. It is far, far better to allow the experience to express itself in order that the entity may then make fuller use of this catalyst.

QUESTIONER: How can an individual assess what energy centers within its being are activated and in no immediate need of attention and which energy centers are not activated and are in need of immediate attention?

RA: I am Ra. The thoughts of an entity, its feelings or emotions, and least of all its behavior are the signposts for the teaching/learning of self by self. In the analysis of one's experiences of a diurnal cycle an entity may assess what it considers to be inappropriate thoughts, behaviors, feelings, and emotions.

In examining these inappropriate activities of mind, body, and spirit complexes the entity may then place these distortions in the proper vibrational ray and thus see where work is needed.

QUESTIONER: In the last session you said, "that when the self is conscious to a great enough extent of the workings of the catalyst of fasting, and the techniques of programming, it then may through concentration of the will and the faculty of faith alone cause reprogramming without the analogy of fasting, diet, or other analogous bodily complex disciplines." What are the techniques of programming which the Higher Self uses to insure that the desired lessons are learned or attempted by the third-density self?

RA: I am Ra. There is but one technique for this growing or nurturing of will and faith, and that is the focusing of the attention. The attention span of those you call children is considered short. The spiritual attention span of most of your peoples is that of the child. Thus it is a matter of wishing to become able to collect one's attention and hold it upon the desired programming.

This, when continued, strengthens the will. The entire activity can only occur when there exists faith that an outcome of this discipline is possible.

QUESTIONER: Can you mention some exercises for helping to increase the attention span?

RA: I am Ra. Such exercises are common among the many mystical traditions of your entities. The visualization of a shape and color which is of personal inspirational quality to the meditator is the heart of what you would call the religious aspects of this sort of visualization.

The visualization of simple shapes and colors which have no innate inspirational quality to the entity form the basis for what you may call your magical traditions.

Whether you image the rose or the circle is not important. However, it is suggested that one or the other path towards visualization be chosen in order to exercise this faculty. This is due to the careful arrangement of shapes and colors which have been described as visualizations by those steeped in the magical tradition.

QUESTIONER: As a youth I was trained in the engineering sciences which include the necessity for three-dimensional visualization for the processes of design. Would this be helpful as a foundation for the type of visualization which you are speaking of, or would it be of no value?

RA: I am Ra. To you, the questioner, this experience was valuable. To a less sensitized entity it would not gain the proper increase of concentrative energy.

QUESTIONER: Then the less sensitized entity should use . . . What should he use for the proper energy?

RA: I am Ra. In the less sensitized individual the choosing of personally inspirational images is appropriate whether this inspiration be the rose which is of perfect beauty, the cross which is of perfect sacrifice, the Buddha which is the All-Being in One, or whatever else may inspire the individual.

QUESTIONER: Using the teach/learning relationship of parent to child, what type of actions would demonstrate the activation of the energy centers in sequence from red to violet?

RA: I am Ra. This shall be the last full query of this working.

The entity, child or adult, as you call it, is not an instrument to be played. The appropriate teach/learning device of parent to child is the open-hearted beingness of the parent and the total acceptance of the beingness of the child. This will encompass whatever material the child entity has brought into the life experience in this plane.

There are two things especially important in this relationship other than the basic acceptance of the child by the parent. Firstly, the experience of whatever means the parent uses to worship and give thanksgiving to the One Infinite Creator, should if possible be shared with the child entity upon a daily basis, as you would say. Secondly, the compassion of parent to child may well be tempered by the understanding that the child entity shall learn the biases of service-to-others or service-to-self from the parental other-self. This is the reason that some discipline is appropriate in the teach/learning. This does not apply to the activation of any one energy center for each entity is unique and each relationship with self and other-self doubly unique. The guidelines given are only general for this reason.

Is there a brief query before we leave this instrument?

QUESTIONER: Is there anything that we can do to make the instrument more comfortable or to improve the contact?

RA: I am Ra. The instrument is well. I leave you, my friends, in the love and the light of the Infinite Creator. Go forth, then, rejoicing in the power and the peace of the One Infinite Creator. Adonai.

Session 43,
March 24, 1981

RA: I am Ra. I greet you in the love and in the light of the One Infinite Creator.

Before we communicate may we request the adjustment, without the touching of this instrument's physical body complex, of the item which presses upon the instrument's head. This is causing some interference with our contact.

QUESTIONER: Is that the pillow or something else? Do you speak of the pillow under the neck?

RA: I am Ra. There is a line of interference crossing the crown of the head.

QUESTIONER: Is it this? (A two inch fold in the sheet is located three inches from the crown of the instrument's head and is laid flat on the bed.) Is that it?

RA: I am Ra. This is correct. Please increase the distance from the crown of the head.

QUESTIONER: (Ruffles in the sheet are smoothed all along the length of the sheet next to the instrument's head.) Is this satisfactory?

RA: I am Ra. Yes.

QUESTIONER: I am sorry that we failed to notice that.

RA: We communicate now.

QUESTIONER: I don't know if it is of any importance, but it occurred to me that the parts removed from the cattle mutilations are the same every time, and I wondered if this is related to the energy centers and why they were important if that was so?

RA: I am Ra. This is basically correct if you may understand that there is a link between energy centers and various thought-forms. Thus the fears of the mass consciousness create the climate for the concentration upon the removal of bodily parts which symbolize areas of concern or fear in the mass consciousness.

QUESTIONER: Are you saying, then, that these parts that are removed are related to the mass consciousness of the third-density human form and that this fear is being used in some way by the thought-form entities in these mutilations?

RA: I am Ra. This is correct. The thought-form entities feed upon fear; thus they are able to do precise damage according to systems of symbology. The other second-density types of which you speak need the, what you call, blood.

QUESTIONER: These other second-density types need the blood to remain in the physical? Do they come in and out of our physical from one of the lower astral planes?

RA: I am Ra. These entities are, shall we say, creatures of the Orion group. They do not exist in astral planes as do the thought-forms but wait within the Earth's surface. We, as always, remind you that it is our impression that this type of information is unimportant.

QUESTIONER: I agree with you wholeheartedly, but I sometimes am at a loss before investigation into an area as to whether it is going to lead to a better understanding. This just seemed to be related somehow to the energy centers which we had been speaking of.

I am going to make a statement and have you comment on it for its correctness. The statement is: When the Creator's light is split or divided into colors and energy centers for experience, then in order to reunite with the Creator the energy centers must be balanced exactly the same as the split light was as it originated from the Creator. Is this correct?

RA: I am Ra. To give this query a simple answer would be nearly impossible.

We shall simplify by concentrating upon what we consider to be the central idea towards which you are striving. We have, many times now, spoken about the relative importance of balancing as opposed to the relative unimportance of maximal activation of each energy center. The reason is as you have correctly surmised. Thusly the entity is concerned, if it be upon the path of positive harvestability, with the regularizing of the various energies of experience. Thus the most fragile entity may be more balanced than one with extreme energy and activity in service-to-others due to the fastidiousness with which the will is focused upon the use of experience in knowing the self. The densities beyond your own give the minimally balanced individual much time/space and space/time with which to continue to refine these inner balances.

QUESTIONER: In the next density, the fourth density, is the catalyst of physical pain used as a mechanism for experiential balancing?

RA: I am Ra. The use of physical pain is minimal, having only to do with the end of the fourth-density incarnation. This physical pain would not be considered severe enough to treat, shall we say, in third density. The catalysts of mental and spiritual pain are used in fourth density.

QUESTIONER: Why is physical pain a part of the end of fourth density?

RA: I am Ra. You would call this variety of pain weariness.

QUESTIONER: Can you state the average lifespan in the fourth density of space/time incarnation?

RA: I am Ra. The space/time incarnation typical of harmonious fourth density is approximately 90,000 of your years as you measure time.

QUESTIONER: Are there multiple incarnations in fourth density with time/space experiences in between incarnations?

RA: I am Ra. This is correct.

QUESTIONER: How long is a cycle of experience in fourth density in our years?

RA: The cycle of experience is approximately 30 million of your years if the entities are not capable of being harvested sooner. There is in this density a harvest which is completely the function of the readiness of the social memory complex. It is not structured as is your own, for it deals with a more transparent distortion of the One Infinite Creator.

QUESTIONER: Then the big difference in harvestability between third and fourth density is that at the end of the third density the individual is harvested as a function of individual violet ray, but it is the violet ray for the entire social memory complex that must be of a harvestable nature to graduate to the fifth density. Is this correct?

RA: I am Ra. This is correct, although in fifth density entities may choose to learn as a social memory complex or as mind/body/spirit complexes and may graduate to sixth density under these conditions, for the wisdom density is an extremely free density whereas the lessons of compassion leading to wisdom necessarily have to do with other-selves.

QUESTIONER: Then is sixth-density harvest strictly of a social memory complex nature because again we have wisdom and compassion blended back using wisdom?

RA: I am Ra. This is quite correct.

QUESTIONER: The physical vehicle that is used in fourth-density space/time is, I am assuming, quite similar to the one that is now used in third density. Is this correct?

RA: I am Ra. The chemical elements used are not the same. However, the appearance is similar.

QUESTIONER: Is it necessary to eat food in fourth density?

RA: I am Ra. This is correct.

QUESTIONER: The mechanism of, shall we say, social catalyst due to a necessity for feeding the body then is active in fourth density. Is this correct?

RA: I am Ra. This is incorrect. The fourth-density being desires to serve and the preparation of foodstuffs is extremely simple due to increased communion between entity and living foodstuff. Therefore, this is not a significant catalyst but rather a simple precondition of the space/time experience. The catalyst involved is the necessity for the ingestion of foodstuffs. This is not considered to be of importance by fourth-density entities and it, therefore, aids in the teach/learning of patience.

QUESTIONER: Could you expand a little bit on how that aids in the teach/learning of patience?

RA: I am Ra. To stop the functioning of service-to-others long enough to ingest foodstuffs is to invoke patience.

QUESTIONER: I'm guessing that it is not necessary to ingest foodstuffs in fifth density. Is this correct?

RA: I am Ra. This is incorrect. However, the vehicle needs food which may be prepared by thought.

QUESTIONER: What type of food would this be?

RA: I am Ra. You would call this type of food, nectar or ambrosia, or a light broth of golden white hue.

QUESTIONER: What is the purpose of ingesting food in fifth density?

RA: I am Ra. This is a somewhat central point. The purpose of space/time is the increase in catalytic action appropriate to the density. One of the preconditions for space/time existence is some form of body complex. Such a body complex must be fueled in some way.

QUESTIONER: In third density the fueling of our bodily complex is not only simply fueling of the bodily complex but gives us opportunities to learn service. In fourth density it not only fuels the complex but gives us opportunities to learn patience. In fifth density it fuels the complex but does it teach?

RA: I am Ra. In fifth density it is comfort for those of like mind gathered together to share in this broth, thus becoming one in light and wisdom while joining hearts and hands in physical activity. Thus in this density it becomes a solace rather than a catalyst for learning.

QUESTIONER: I am simply trying to trace the evolution of this catalyst that then, as you say, changes in fifth density. I might as well complete this and ask if there is any ingestion of food in sixth density?

RA: I am Ra. This is correct. However, the nature of this food is that of light and is impossible to describe to you in any meaningful way as regards the thrust of your query.

QUESTIONER: On this planet after the harvest is complete, will fourth-density beings be incarnate on the surface as we know it now?

RA: I am Ra. The probability/possibility vortices indicate this to be most likely.

QUESTIONER: Then will there be at that time any fifth-density or sixth-density beings on the surface of the planet?

RA: I am Ra. Not for a fairly long measure of your time as fourth-density beings need to spend their learn/teaching space/time with their own density's entities.

QUESTIONER: Then basically what you are saying is that at that point the teachings of fifth- or sixth-density beings would not be too well understood by the new fourth-density beings?

RA: I am Ra. Do you wish to query us upon this point?

QUESTIONER: I guess I didn't state that correctly. Would the new fourth-density beings then need to evolve in their thinking to reach a point where fifth-density lessons would be of value?

RA: I am Ra. We grasp the thrust of your query. Although it is true that as fourth-density beings progress they have more and more need for other density teachings, it is also true that just as we speak to you due to the calling, so the information called is always available. It is simply that fifth-density beings will not live upon the surface of the planetary sphere until the planet reaches fifth-density vibratory level.

QUESTIONER: I was wondering, then, if the mechanism of teach/learning was the same relatively then in fourth density. From what you say, it is necessary first for a call to exist for the teach/learning of fifth density to be given to fourth just as a call must exist here before fourth-density lessons are given to third density. Is this correct?

RA: I am Ra. This query is misguided, for experience in fourth density is emphatically not the same as third-density experience. However, it is correct that the same mechanism of calling predisposes the information received in a way consonant with free will.

You may ask one more full question at this working.

QUESTIONER: You stated that the key to strengthening the will is concentration. Can you tell me the relative importance of the following aids to concentration? I have listed: silence, temperature control, comfort of body, screening as a Faraday cage would screen electromagnetic radiation, visible light screening, and a constant smell such as the use of incense. In other words, an isolation-type of situation. You mentioned that this was one of the functions of the pyramid.

RA: I am Ra. The analogies of body complex to mind and spirit complex activities have been discussed previously. You may consider all of these aforementioned aids as those helpful to the stimulation of that which in actuality aids concentration, that being the will of the entity. This free will may be focused at any object or goal.

QUESTIONER: I was really trying to get at whether it would be of great importance to construct a better place for our meditations. We have distractions here of the types which I mentioned, and I know that it is a function of our total free will as to whether we construct this or not, but I was trying to get at the principles behind and the relative importance of the Faraday cage. It would be quite a construction and I was wondering if it would be of any real value?

RA: I am Ra. Without infringing upon free will we feel it possible to state that the Faraday cage and the isolation tank are gadgets.

The surrounding of self in a sylvan atmosphere, apart from distractions, in a place of working used for no other purpose, in which you and your associates agree to lay aside all goals but that of the meditative seeking of the Infinite Creator is, shall we say, not gadgetry but the making use of the creation of the Father in second-density love, and in the love and support of other-selves. Are there any brief queries before this working is at an end?

QUESTIONER: Is there anything that we can do to make the instrument more comfortable or to improve the contact?

RA: I am Ra. All is well. I leave you in the love and the light of the One Infinite Creator. Go forth, therefore, rejoicing in the power and the peace of the One Infinite Creator. Adonai.

SESSION 44, MARCH 28,1981, AND SESSION 45, APRIL 6, 1981, CONTAIN
ONLY PERSONAL MATERIAL AND WERE, FOR THAT REASON, REMOVED.

Session 46,
April 15, 1981

RA: I am Ra. I greet you in the love and in the light of the One Infinite Creator. We communicate now.

QUESTIONER: If an entity polarizes toward the service-to-self path, would anger have the same physical effect that it would have on the entity polarizing on the service-to-others path? Would it also cause cancer, or is it just a catalytic effect working in the positively polarizing entity?

RA: I am Ra. The catalytic mechanisms are dependent, not upon the chosen polarity of a mind/body/spirit complex, but upon the use or purpose to which this catalyst is put. Thus the entity which uses the experience of anger to polarize consciously positively or negatively does not experience the bodily catalyst but rather uses the catalyst in mental configuration.

QUESTIONER: I am not sure that I understand that. Let's take some examples: an entity polarizing toward the negative path becomes angry. Let's take the condition where he develops a cancer. What is the principle that is at work for him?

RA I am Ra. We see the thrust of your query and will respond at variance with the specific query if that meets with your approval.

QUESTIONER: Certainly.

RA: The entity polarizing positively perceives the anger. This entity, if using this catalyst mentally, blesses and loves this anger in itself. It then intensifies this anger consciously in mind alone until the folly of this red-ray energy is perceived not as folly in itself but as energy subject to spiritual entropy due to the randomness of energy being used.

Positive orientation then provides the will and faith to continue this mentally intense experience of letting the anger be understood, accepted, and integrated with the mind/body/spirit complex. The other-self which is the object of anger is thus transformed into an object of acceptance, understanding, and accommodation, all being reintegrated using the great energy which anger began.

The negatively oriented mind/body/spirit complex will use this anger in a similarly conscious fashion, refusing to accept the undirected or random energy of anger and instead, through will and faith, funneling this energy into a practical means of venting the negative aspect of this emotion so as to obtain control over other-self, or otherwise control the situation causing anger.

Control is the key to negatively polarized use of catalyst. Acceptance is the key to positively polarized use of catalyst. Between these polarities lies the potential for this random and undirected energy creating a bodily complex analog of what you call the cancerous growth of tissue.

QUESTIONER: Then as I understand it you are saying that if the positively polarizing entity fails to accept the other-self or if the negatively polarizing entity fails to control the other-self, either of these conditions will cause cancer, possibly. Is this correct?

RA: I am Ra. This is partially correct. The first acceptance, or control depending upon polarity, is of the self. Anger is one of many things to be accepted and loved as a part of self or controlled as a part of self, if the entity is to do work.

QUESTIONER: Then are you saying that if a negatively polarizing entity is unable to control his own anger or unable to control himself in anger that he may cause cancer? Is this correct?

RA: I am Ra. This is quite correct. The negative polarization contains a great requirement for control and repression.

QUESTIONER: A repression of what?

RA: I am Ra. Any mind complex distortion which you may call emotional which is of itself disorganized, needs, in order to be useful to the negatively oriented entity, to be repressed and then brought to the surface in an organized use. Thus you may find for instance, negatively polarized entities controlling and repressing such basic bodily complex needs as the sexual desire in order that in the practice thereof the will may be used to enforce itself upon the other-self with greater efficiency when the sexual behavior is allowed.

QUESTIONER: Then the positively oriented entity, rather than attempting repression of emotion, would balance the emotion as stated in an earlier contact. Is this correct?

RA: I am Ra. This is correct and illustrates the path of unity.

QUESTIONER: Then cancer is a training catalyst operating for both polarities in approximately the same way but creating or attempting to create polarization in both directions, positive and negative, depending upon the orientation of the entity experiencing the catalyst. Is this correct?

RA: I am Ra. This is incorrect in that catalyst is unconscious and does not work with intelligence but rather is part of the, shall we say, mechanism of learn/teaching set up by the sub-Logos before the beginning of your space/time.

QUESTIONER: How does cancer do this learn/teaching when the entity developing cancer has no conscious idea of what is happening to him when he develops cancer?

RA: I am Ra. In many cases catalyst is not used.

QUESTIONER: What is the plan for use of the catalyst of cancer?

RA: I am Ra. The catalyst, and all catalyst, is designed to offer experience. This experience in your density may be loved and accepted or it may be controlled. These are the two paths. When neither path is chosen the catalyst fails in its design and the entity proceeds until catalyst strikes it which causes it to form a bias towards acceptance and love or separation and control. There is no lack of space/time in which this catalyst may work.

QUESTIONER: I am assuming that the plan of the Logos is for positively and negatively polarized social memory complexes in fourth density and above. Can you tell me the purpose of the plan for these two types of social memory complexes with respect to Coulomb's Law or negative and positive electrical polarity, or in any way that you can?

RA: I am Ra. This instrument grows weary. We shall speak with you again. We may indicate the possibility, without further harm to this instrument, of approximately two sessions per your weekly period until these weeks of potential for attack and presence of very low physical energy are passed. May we say it is good to be with this group. We appreciate your fidelity. Are there any brief queries before the end of this work time?

QUESTIONER: Only is there anything that we can do to make the instrument more comfortable or to improve the contact?

RA: I am Ra. Each is supporting the instrument well and the instrument remains steady in its purpose. You are conscientious. All is well. We ward you ware of any laxity regarding the arrangement and orientation of appurtenances.

I am Ra. I leave you, my friends, in the love and in the light of the One Infinite Creator. Go forth, therefore, rejoicing in the power and the peace of the One Infinite Creator. Adonai.

Session 47,
April 18, 1981

RA: I am Ra. I greet you in the love and in the light of the One Infinite Creator. We communicate now.

QUESTIONER: Could you first give us an indication of the condition of the instrument?

RA: I am Ra. It is as previously stated.

QUESTIONER: The question that I was trying to ask at the end of the last session was: Of what value to evolution or experience with respect to the Creator knowing Itself are the positive and negative social memory complexes that form starting in fourth density, and why was this planned by the Logos?

RA: I am Ra. There are inherent incorrectness in your query. However, we may answer the main point of it.

The incorrectness lies in the consideration that social memory complexes were planned by the Logos or sub-Logos. This is incorrect, as the unity of the Creator exists within the smallest portion of any material created by Love, much less in a self-aware being.

However, the distortion of free will causes the social memory complex to appear as a possibility at a certain stage of evolution of mind. The purpose, or consideration which causes entities to form such complexes, of these social memory complexes, is a very simple extension of the basic distortion towards the Creator's knowing of Itself, for when a group of mind/body/spirits becomes able to form a social memory complex, all experience of each entity is available to the whole of the complex. Thus the Creator knows more of Its creation in each entity partaking of this communion of entities.

QUESTIONER: You gave the values of better than 50 percent

service-to-others for fourth-density positive and better than 95 percent service-to-self for fourth-density negative social memory
complexes. Do these two values correspond to the same rate, shall I
say, of vibration?

RA: I am Ra. I perceive you have difficulty in expressing your query.
We shall respond in an attempt to clarify your query.

The vibratory rates are not to be understood as the same in positive and negative orientations. They are to be understood as having
the power to accept and work with intelligent infinity to a certain
degree or intensity. Due to the fact that the primary color, shall we
say, or energy blue is missing from the negatively oriented system of
power, the green/blue vibratory energies are not seen in the vibratory
schedules or patterns of negative fourth and fifth rates of
vibration.

The positive on the other hand, shall we say, has the full spectrum of true color time/space vibratory patterns and thus contains
a variant vibratory pattern or schedule. Each is capable of doing
fourth-density work. This is the criterion for harvest.

QUESTIONER: Did you say that blue was missing from fourth-density negative?

RA: I am Ra. Let us clarify further. As we have previously stated, all
beings have the potential for all possible vibratory rates. Thus the
potential of the green and blue energy center activation is, of course,
precisely where it must be in a creation of Love. However, the negatively polarized entity will have achieved harvest due to extremely
efficient use of red and yellow/orange, moving directly to the gateway
indigo bringing through this intelligent energy channel the instreamings of intelligent infinity.

QUESTIONER: Then at fourth-density graduation into fifth is there
anything like that which you gave as the percentages necessary for
third-density graduation into fourth in polarization?

RA: I am Ra. There are, in your modes of thinking, responses we can
make, which we shall make. However, the important point is that the
graduations from density to density do occur. The positive/negative
polarity is a thing which will, at the sixth level, simply become history.
Therefore, we speak in an illusory time continuum when we discuss
statistics of positive versus negative harvest into fifth. A large
percentage of fourth-density negative entities continue the negative

path from fourth to fifth-density experience, for without wisdom the compassion and desire to aid other-self is not extremely well informed. Thus though one loses approximately two percent moving from negative to positive during the fourth-density experience we find approximately eight percent of graduations into fifth density those of the negative.

QUESTIONER: What I was actually asking was if 50 percent is required for graduation from third to fourth in the positive sense and 95 percent was required for graduation in the negative sense, does this have to more closely approach 100 percent for graduation in both cases for graduation from fourth to fifth density? Does an entity have to be 99 percent polarized for negative and maybe 80 percent polarized positive for graduation?

RA: I am Ra. We perceive the query now.

To give this in your terms is misleading for there are, shall we say, visual aids or training aids available in fourth density which automatically aid the entity in polarization while cutting down extremely upon the quick effect of catalyst. Thus the density above yours must take up more space/time.

The percentage of service-to-others of positively oriented entities will harmoniously approach 98 percent in intention. The qualifications for fifth density, however, involve understanding. This then, becomes the primary qualification for graduation from fourth to fifth density. To achieve this graduation the entity must be able to understand the actions, the movements, and the dance. There is no percentage describable which measures this understanding. It is a measure of efficiency of perception. It may be measured by light. The ability to love, accept, and use a certain intensity of light thus creates the requirement for both positive and negative fourth to fifth harvesting.

QUESTIONER: Can you define what you mean by a "crystallized entity"?

RA: I am Ra. We have used this particular term because it has a fairly precise meaning in your language. When a crystalline structure is formed of your physical material the elements present in each molecule are bonded in a regularized fashion with elements in each other molecule. Thus the structure is regular and, when fully and perfectly crystallized, has certain properties. It will not splinter or break; it is very strong without effort; and it is radiant, traducing light into a beautiful refraction giving pleasure of the eye to many.

QUESTIONER: In our esoteric literature numerous bodies are listed. I have listed here the physical body, the etheric, the emotional, the astral. Can you tell me if this listing is the proper number, and can you tell me the uses and purposes and effects etc., of each of these and any other bodies that may be in our mind/body/spirit complex?

RA: I am Ra. To answer your query fully would be the work of many sessions such as this one, for the interrelationships of the various bodies and each body's effects in various situations is an enormous study. However, we shall begin by referring your minds back to the spectrum of true colors and the usage of this understanding in grasping the various densities of your octave.

We have the number seven repeated from the macrocosm to the microcosm in structure and experience. Therefore, it would only be expected that there would be seven basic bodies which we would perhaps be most lucid by stating as red-ray body, etc. However, we are aware that you wish to correspond these bodies mentioned with the color rays. This will be confusing, for various teachers have offered their teach/learning understanding in various terms. Thus one may name a subtle body one thing and another find a different name.

The red-ray body is your chemical body. However, it is not the body which you have as clothing in the physical. It is the unconstructed material of the body, the elemental body without form. This basic unformed material body is important to understand for there are healings which may be carried out by the simple understanding of the elements present in the physical vehicle.

The orange-ray body is the physical body complex. This body complex is still not the body you inhabit but rather the body formed without self-awareness, the body in the womb before the spirit/mind complex enters. This body may live without the inhabitation of the mind and spirit complexes. However, it seldom does so.

The yellow-ray body is your physical vehicle which you know of at this time and in which you experience catalyst. This body has the mind/body/spirit characteristics and is equal to the physical illusion, as you have called it.

The green-ray body is that body which may be seen in séance when what you call ectoplasm is furnished. This is a lighter body packed more densely with life. You may call this the astral body following some other teachings. Others have called this same body the etheric body. However, this is not correct in the sense that the etheric body is that body of gateway wherein intelligent energy is able to mold the mind/body/spirit complex.

The light body or blue-ray body may be called the devachanic body. There are many other names for this body especially in your so-called Indian Sutras or writings, for there are those among these peoples which have explored these regions and understand the various types of devachanic bodies. There are many, many types of bodies in each density, much like your own.

The indigo-ray body which we choose to call the etheric body is, as we have said, the gateway body. In this body form is substance and you may only see this body as that of light as it may mold itself as it desires.

The violet-ray body may perhaps be understood as what you might call the Buddha body or that body which is complete.

Each of these bodies has an effect upon your mind/body/spirit complex in your life beingness. The interrelationships, as we have said, are many and complex.

Perhaps one suggestion that may be indicated is this: The indigo-ray body may be used by the healer once the healer becomes able to place its consciousness in this etheric state. The violet-ray or Buddhic body is of equal efficacy to the healer for within it lies a sense of wholeness which is extremely close to unity with all that there is. These bodies are part of each entity and the proper use of them and understanding of them is, though far advanced from the standpoint of third-density harvest, nevertheless useful to the adept.

QUESTIONER: Which bodies do we have immediately after physical death from this yellow-ray body that I now am in?

RA: I am Ra. You have all bodies in potentiation.

QUESTIONER: Then the yellow-ray body in potentiation is used to create this chemical arrangement that I have as a physical body now. Is this correct?

RA: I am Ra. This is incorrect only in that in your present incarnation the yellow-ray body is not in potentiation but in activation, it being that body which is manifest.

QUESTIONER: Then after death from this incarnation we still have the yellow-ray body in potentiation, but then in the general case of our planetary population after death, would they then normally have the green-ray body manifested?

RA: I am Ra. Not immediately. The first body which activates itself upon death is the "form-maker" or the indigo-ray body. This body remains—you have called it the "ka"—until etherea has been penetrated and understanding has been gained by the mind/body/spirit totality. Once this is achieved, if the proper body to be activated is green ray, then this will occur.

QUESTIONER: Let me make a statement and you tell me if I am correct. After death then, if an entity is unaware, he may become what is called an earthbound spirit until he is able to achieve the required awareness for activation of one of his bodies. Would it be possible then to activate any of the bodies from red through violet?

RA: I am Ra. Given the proper stimulus, this is correct.

QUESTIONER: What stimulus would create what we call an earthbound spirit or a lingering ghost?

RA: I am Ra. The stimulus for this is the faculty of the will. If the will of yellow-ray mind/body/spirit is that which is stronger than the progressive impetus of the physical death towards realization of that which comes, that is, if the will is concentrated enough upon the previous experience, the entity's shell of yellow ray, though no longer activated, cannot either be completely deactivated and, until the will is released, the mind/body/spirit complex is caught. This often occurs, as we see you are aware, in the case of sudden death as well as in the case of extreme concern for a thing or an other-self.

QUESTIONER: Well then, does orange-ray activation after death occur very frequently with this planet?

RA: I am Ra. Quite infrequently, due to the fact that this particular manifestation is without will. Occasionally an other-self will so demand the form of the one passing through the physical death that some semblance of the being will remain. This is orange ray. This is rare, for normally if one entity desires another enough to call it, the entity will have the corresponding desire to be called. Thus the manifestation would be the shell of yellow ray.

QUESTIONER: What does the large percentage of the Earth's population, as they pass through the physical, activate?

RA: I am Ra. This shall be the last full query of this working.

The normal procedure, given an harmonious passage from yellow-ray bodily manifestation, is for the mind and spirit complex to rest in the etheric or indigo body until such time as the entity begins its preparation for experience in an incarnated place which has a manifestation formed by the etheric energy molding it into activation and manifestation. This indigo body, being intelligent energy, is able to offer the newly dead, as you would term it, soul a perspective and a place from which to view the experience most recently manifested. Is there a short query we may answer at this time?

QUESTIONER: I will only ask if there is anything that we may do to make the instrument more comfortable or to improve the contact?

RA: I am Ra. The appurtenances are conscientiously measured by eye and spirit. You are conscientious. All is well. Observe this instrument to ensure continued building of the vital energies. It will have to work upon its own physical energies for this weakness was brought about by free will of the self.

I am Ra. We leave you now in the love and in the light of the One Infinite Creator. Go forth, therefore, rejoicing in the power and in the peace of the One Infinite Creator. Adonai.

Session 48,
April 22, 1981

RA: I am Ra. I greet you in the love and in the light of the One Infinite Creator. We communicate now.

QUESTIONER: Could you tell us of the instrument's condition and if she is improving with time?

RA: I am Ra. This instrument's vital energies are improving with time, as you measure it. This instrument's physical energies are less than your previous asking.

QUESTIONER: Thank you. If you, Ra, as an individualized entity were incarnate on Earth now with full awareness and memory of what you know now, what would be your objective at this time on Earth as far as activities are concerned?

RA: I am Ra. The query suggests that which has been learned to be impractical. However, were we to again be naive enough to think that our physical presence was any more effective than that love/light we send your peoples and the treasure of this contact, we would do as we did do. We would be, and we would offer our selves as teach/learners.

QUESTIONER: My lecture yesterday was attended by only a few. If this had occurred during a UFO flap many more would have attended. Since Orion entities cause the flaps, what is Orion's reward for visibility in that they actually create greater opportunities for the dissemination of information such as this information at those times?

RA: I am Ra. This assumption is incorrect. The flaps cause many fears among your peoples, many speakings, understandings concerning plots, cover-ups, mutilations, killings, and other negative impressions. Even those supposedly positive reports which gain public awareness speak of doom. You may understand yourself as one who will be in the minority due to the understandings which you wish to share, if we may use that misnomer.

We perceive there is a further point we may posit at this time. The audience brought about by Orion-type publicity is not seeded by seniority of vibration to a great extent. The audiences receiving teach/learnings without stimulus from publicity will be more greatly oriented towards illumination. Therefore, forget you the counting.

QUESTIONER: Thank you. That clears up that point very well.

Can you tell me how positive and negative polarizations in fourth and fifth density are used to cause working in consciousness?

RA: I am Ra. There is very little work in consciousness in fourth and in fifth densities compared to the work done in third density. The work that is accomplished in positive fourth is that work whereby the positive social memory complex, having, through slow stages, harmoniously integrated itself, goes forth to aid those of less positive orientation which seek their aid. Thus their service is their work and through this dynamic between the societal self and the other-self, which is the object of love, greater and greater intensities of understanding or compassion are attained. This intensity continues until the appropriate intensity of the light may be welcomed. This is fourth-density harvest.

Within fourth-density positive there are minor amounts of catalyst of a spiritual and mental complex distortion. This occurs during the process of harmonizing to the extent of forming the social memory complex. This causes some small catalyst and work to occur, but the great work of fourth density lies in the contact betwixt the societal self and less polarized other-self.

In fourth-density negative much work is accomplished during the fighting for position which precedes the period of the social memory complex. There are opportunities to polarize negatively by control of other-selves. During the social memory complex period of fourth-density negative the situation is the same. The work takes place through the societal reaching out to less polarized other-self in order to aid in negative polarization.

In fifth-density positive and negative the concept of work done through a potential difference is not particularly helpful as fifth-density entities are, again, intensifying rather than potentiating.

In positive, the fifth-density complex uses sixth-density teach/learners to study the more illuminated understandings of unity thus becoming more and more wise. Fifth-density positive social memory complexes will choose to divide their service to others in two ways: first, the beaming of light to creation; second, the sending of groups to be of aid as instruments of light such as those whom you are familiar with through channels.

In fifth-density negative, service to self has become extremely intense and the self has shrunk or compacted so that the dialogues with the teach/learners are used exclusively in order to intensify wisdom. There are very, very few fifth-density negative Wanderers for they fear the forgetting. There are very, very few fifth-density Orion members for they do not any longer perceive any virtue in other-selves.

QUESTIONER: Thank you. I would like to take as an example an entity, starting before birth, who is roughly high on the seniority list for positive polarization and possible harvestability at the end of this cycle and follow a full cycle of his experience starting before his incarnation—which body is activated, the process of becoming incarnate, the activation of the third-density physical body, the process as the body moves through this density and is acted upon by catalysts, the process of death, and the activation of the various bodies so that we make a full circuit from a point prior to incarnation back around through incarnation and death; you might say one cycle of incarnation in this density. Could you do that for me?

RA: I am Ra. Your query is most distorted for it assumes that creations are alike. Each mind/body/spirit complex has its own patterns of activation and its own rhythms of awakening. The important thing for harvest is the harmonious balance between the various energy centers of the mind/body/spirit complex. This is to be noted as of relative import. We grasp the thrust of your query and will make a most general answer stressing the unimportance of such arbitrary generalizations.

The entity, before incarnation, dwells in the appropriate, shall we say, place in time/space. The true color type of this location will be dependent upon the entity's needs. Those entities for instance which, being Wanderers, have the green, blue, or indigo true color core of mind/body/spirit complex will have rested therein.

Entrance into incarnation requires the investment or activation of the indigo ray or etheric body for this is the "form-maker." The young or small physical mind/body/spirit complex has the seven energy centers potentiated before the birthing process. There are also analogs in time/space of these energy centers corresponding to the seven energy centers in each of the seven true color densities. Thus in the microcosm exists all the experience that is prepared. It is as though the infant contains the universe.

The patterns of activation of an entity of high seniority will undoubtedly move with some rapidity to the green-ray level which is the springboard to primary blue. There is always some difficulty in penetrating blue primary energy for it requires that which your people have in great paucity; that is, honesty. Blue ray is the ray of free communication with self and with other-self. Having accepted that an harvestable or nearly harvestable entity will be working from this green-ray springboard one may then posit that the experiences in the remainder of the incarnation will be focused upon activation of the primary blue ray of freely given communication, of indigo ray, that of freely shared intelligent energy, and if possible, moving through this gateway, the penetration of violet-ray intelligent infinity. This may be seen to be manifested by a sense of the consecrate or hallowed nature of everyday creations and activities.

Upon the bodily complex death, as you call this transition, the entity will immediately, upon realization of its state, return to the indigo form-maker body and rest therein until the proper future placement is made.

Here we have the anomaly of harvest. In harvest the entity will then transfer its indigo body into violet-ray manifestation as seen in true color yellow. This is for the purpose of gauging the harvestability of the entity. After this anomalous activity has been carefully completed, the entity will move into indigo body again and be placed in the correct true color locus in space/time and time/space at which time the healings and learn/teachings necessary shall be completed and further incarnation needs determined.

QUESTIONER: Who supervises the determination of further incarnation needs and sets up the seniority list for incarnation?

RA: I am Ra. This is a query with two answers.

Firstly, there are those directly under the Guardians who are responsible for the incarnation patterns of those incarnating automatically, that is, without conscious self-awareness of the process of spiritual evolution. You may call these beings angelic if you prefer. They are, shall we say, "local" or of your planetary sphere.

The seniority of vibration is to be likened unto placing various grades of liquids in the same glass. Some will rise to the top; others will sink to the bottom. Layers and layers of entities will ensue. As harvest draws near, those filled with the most light and love will naturally, and without supervision, be in line, shall we say, for the experience of incarnation.

When the entity becomes aware in its mind/body/spirit complex totality of the mechanism for spiritual evolution it, itself, will arrange and place those lessons and entities necessary for maximum growth and expression of polarity in the incarnative experience before the forgetting process occurs. The only disadvantage of this total free will of those senior entities choosing the manner of incarnation experiences is that some entities attempt to learn so much during one incarnative experience that the intensity of catalyst disarranges the polarized entity and the experience thus is not maximally useful as intended.

QUESTIONER: An analogy to that would be a student in college signing up for more courses than he could possibly assimilate in the time they were given. Is this correct?

RA: I am Ra. This is correct.

QUESTIONER: Could you tell me how the various bodies, red through violet, are linked to the energy centers, red through violet? Are they linked in some way?

RA: I am Ra. This shall be the last full query of this working.

As we have noted, each of the true color densities has the seven energy centers and each entity contains all this in potentiation. The activation, while in yellow ray, of violet-ray intelligent infinity is a passport to the next octave of experience. There are adepts who have penetrated many, many of the energy centers and several of the true colors. This must be done with utmost care while in the physical body for as we noted when speaking of the dangers of linking red/orange/ yellow circuitry with true color blue circuitry the potential for disarrangement of the mind/body/spirit complex is great. However, the entity who penetrates intelligent infinity is basically capable of walking the universe with unfettered tread.

Is there any brief query before we leave this instrument?

QUESTIONER: Just if there is anything that we can do to make the instrument more comfortable or to improve the contact?

RA: I am Ra. All is well. As we have said, this instrument is weak physically and continued work times will lengthen this weakness. The continued contact also aids in the continued climb in vital energy of the instrument as well as the integration and vital energy of the group as an unit. The choice is yours. We are pleased. All is well. You are conscientious. Continue so.

I am Ra. I leave you in the love and in the light of the One Infinite Creator. Go forth, then, my friends, rejoicing in the power and in the peace of the One Infinite Creator. Adonai.

Session 49,
April 27, 1981

RA: I am Ra. I greet you in the love and in the light of the One Infinite Creator. We communicate now.

QUESTIONER: Would you please give us a reading on the instrument's condition?

RA: I am Ra. It is as previously stated.

QUESTIONER: I was wondering; in a previous session you had mentioned the left and right ear tones, the left and the right brain somehow being related to the polarities of service-to-self and service-to-others. Could you comment on this?

RA: I am Ra. We may comment on this.

QUESTIONER: Will you go ahead and comment on this?

RA: I am Ra. The lobes of your physical complex brain are alike in their use of weak electrical energy. The entity ruled by intuition and impulse is equal to the entity governed by rational analysis when polarity is considered. The lobes may both be used for service to self or service-to-others. It may seem that the rational or analytical mind might have more of a possibility of successfully pursuing the negative orientation due to the fact that in our understanding too much order is by its essence negative. However, this same ability to structure abstract concepts and to analyze experiential data may be the key to rapid positive polarization. It may be said that those whose analytical capacities are predominant have somewhat more to work with in polarizing.

The function of intuition is to inform intelligence. In your illusion the unbridled predominance of intuition will tend to keep an entity from the greater polarizations due to the vagaries of intuitive perception. As you may see, these two types of brain structure need to be balanced in order that the net sum of experiential catalyst will be polarization and illumination, for without the acceptance by the rational mind of the worth of the intuitive faculty the creative aspects which aid in illumination will be stifled.

There is one correspondence between right and left and positive and negative. The web of energy which surrounds your bodies contains somewhat complex polarizations. The left area of the head and upper shoulder is most generally seen to be of a negative polarization whereas the right is of positive polarization, magnetically speaking. This is the cause of the tone's meaning for you.

QUESTIONER: Will you expand on the positive and negative polarizations in general and how they apply to individuals and planets, etc.? I think there is a correlation here, but I'm not sure.

RA: I am Ra. It is correct that there is a correlation between the energy field of an entity of your nature and planetary bodies, for all material is constructed by means of the dynamic tension of the magnetic field. The lines of force in both cases may be seen to be much like the interweaving spirals of the braided hair. Thus positive and negative wind and interweave forming geometric relationships in the energy fields of both persons, as you would call a mind/body/spirit complex, and planets.

The negative pole is the south pole or the lower pole. The north or upper pole is positive. The crisscrossing of these spiraling energies form primary, secondary, and tertiary energy centers. You are familiar with the primary energy centers of the physical, mental, and spiritual body complex. Secondary points of the crisscrossing of positive and negative center orientation revolve about several of your centers. The yellow-ray center may be seen to have secondary energy centers in elbow, in knee, and in the subtle bodies at a slight spacing from the physical vehicle at points describing diamonds about the entity's navel area surrounding the body.

One may examine each of the energy centers for such secondary centers. Some of your peoples work with these energy centers, and you call this acupuncture. However, it is to be noted that there are most often anomalies in the placement of the energy centers so that the scientific precision of this practice is brought into question. Like most scientific attempts at precision, it fails to take into account the unique qualities of each creation.

The most important concept to grasp about the energy field is that the lower or negative pole will draw the universal energy into itself from the cosmos. Therefrom it will move upward to be met and reacted to by the positive spiraling energy moving downward from within. The measure of an entity's level of ray activity is the locus wherein the south pole outer energy has been met by the inner spiraling positive energy.

As an entity grows more polarized this locus will move upwards. This phenomenon has been called by your peoples the kundalini. However, it may better be thought of as the meeting place of cosmic and inner, shall we say, vibratory understanding. To attempt to raise the locus of this meeting without realizing the metaphysical principles of magnetism upon which this depends is to invite great imbalance.

QUESTIONER: What process would be the recommended process for correctly awakening the kundalini and of what value would that be?

RA: I am Ra. The metaphor of the coiled serpent being called upwards is vastly appropriate for consideration by your peoples. This is what you are attempting when you seek. There are, as we have stated, great misapprehensions concerning this metaphor and the nature of pursuing its goal. We must generalize and ask that you grasp the fact that this in effect renders far less useful that which we share. However, as each entity is unique, generalities are our lot when communicating for your possible edification.

We have two types of energy. We are attempting then, as entities in any true color of this octave, to move the meeting place of inner and outer natures further and further along or upward along the energy centers. The two methods of approaching this with sensible method are first, the seating within one's self of those experiences which are attracted to the entity through the south pole. Each experience will need to be observed, experienced, balanced, accepted, and seated within the individual. As the entity grows in self-acceptance and awareness of catalyst the location of the comfortable seating of these experiences will rise to the new true color entity. The experience, whatever it may be, will be seated in red ray and considered as to its survival content and so forth.

Each experience will be sequentially understood by the growing and seeking mind/body/spirit complex in terms of survival, then in terms of personal identity, then in terms of social relations, then in terms of universal love, then in terms of how the experience may beget free communication, then in terms of how the experience may be linked to universal energies, and finally in terms of the sacramental nature of each experience.

Meanwhile the Creator lies within. In the north pole the crown is already upon the head and the entity is potentially a god. This energy is brought into being by the humble and trusting acceptance of this energy through meditation and contemplation of the self and of the Creator.

Where these energies meet is where the serpent will have achieved its height. When this uncoiled energy approaches universal love and radiant being the entity is in a state whereby the harvestability of the entity comes nigh.

QUESTIONER: Will you recommend a technique of meditation?

RA: I am Ra. No.

QUESTIONER: Is it better, or shall I say, does it produce more usable results in meditation to leave the mind as blank as possible and let it run down, so to speak, or is it better to focus in meditation on some object or some thing for concentration?

RA: I am Ra. This shall be the last full query of this work time.

Each of the two types of meditation is useful for a particular reason. The passive meditation involving the clearing of the mind, the emptying of the mental jumble which is characteristic of mind complex activity among your peoples, is efficacious for those whose goal is to achieve an inner silence as a base from which to listen to the Creator. This is an useful and helpful tool and is by far the most generally useful type of meditation as opposed to contemplation or prayer.

The type of meditation which may be called visualization has as its goal not that which is contained in the meditation itself. Visualization is the tool of the adept. Those who learn to hold visual images in mind are developing an inner concentrative power that can transcend boredom and discomfort. When this ability has become crystallized in an adept the adept may then do polarizing in consciousness without external action which can effect the planetary consciousness. This is the reason for the existence of the so-called White Magician. Only those wishing to pursue the conscious raising of planetary vibration will find visualization to be a particularly satisfying type of meditation.

Contemplation or the consideration in a meditative state of an inspiring image or text is extremely useful also among your peoples, and the faculty of will called praying is also of a potentially helpful nature. Whether it is indeed an helpful activity depends quite totally upon the intentions and objects of the one who prays.

May we ask if there are any brief queries at this time?

QUESTIONER: I will just ask if there is anything that we may do to make the instrument more comfortable or to improve the contact and if the two periods per week are still appropriate?

RA: I am Ra. We request your care in the placement of the neck support for this entity as it is too often careless. You are conscientious and your alignments are well. The timing, if we may use that expression, of the sessions is basically correct. However, you are to be commended for observing fatigue in the circle and refraining from a working until all were in love, harmony, and vital energy as one being. This is, and will continue to be, most helpful.

I am Ra. I leave you in the love and in the light of the One Infinite Creator. Go forth, therefore, rejoicing in the power and in the peace of the One Infinite Creator. Adonai.

Session 50,
May 6, 1981

RA: I am Ra. I greet you in the love and in the light of the One Infinite Creator. We communicate now.

QUESTIONER: Could you please give me an indication of the instrument's condition now?

RA: I am Ra. It is as previously stated.

QUESTIONER: In the last session you made the statement that experiences are attracted into the entity through the south pole. Could you expand on that and give us a definition of what you mean?

RA: I am Ra. It takes some consideration to accomplish the proper perspective for grasping the sense of the above information. The south or negative pole is one which attracts. It pulls unto itself those things magnetized to it. So with the mind/body/spirit complex. The in-flow of experience is of the south pole influx. You may consider this a simplistic statement.

The only specific part of this correctness is that the red ray or foundation energy center, being the lowest or root energy center of the physical vehicle, will have the first opportunity to react to any experience. In this way only, you may see a physical locus of the south pole being identified with the root energy center. In every facet of mind and body the root or foundation will be given the opportunity to function first.

What is this opportunity but survival? This is the root possibility of response and may be found to be characteristic of the basic functions of both mind and body. You will find this instinct the strongest, and once this is balanced much is open to the seeker. The south pole then ceases blocking the experiential data and higher energy centers of mind and body become availed of the opportunity to use the experience drawn to it.

QUESTIONER: Why do you say the experience is drawn to or attracted to the entity?

RA: I am Ra. We say this due to our understanding that this is the nature of the phenomenon of experiential catalyst and its entry into the mind/body/spirit complex's awareness.

QUESTIONER: Could you give an example of how an entity sets up a condition for attracting a particular experiential catalyst and how that catalyst then is provided or is learned.

RA: I am Ra. Such an example may be given.

QUESTIONER: Will you give that?

RA: I am Ra. We paused to scan (name's) consciousness to use its experiential catalyst as example. We may proceed.

This is one instance and extrapolation may be made to other entities which are aware of the process of evolution. This entity chose, before incarnation, the means whereby catalyst had great probability of being obtained. This entity desired the process of expressing love and light without expecting any return. This entity programmed also to endeavor to accomplish spiritual work and to comfort itself with companionship in the doing of this work.

Agreements were made prior to incarnation; the first, with the so-called parents and siblings of this entity. This provided the experiential catalyst for the situation of offering radiance of being without expectation of return. The second program involved agreements with several entities. These agreements provided and will provide, in your time/space and space/time continuum, opportunities for the experiential catalyst of work and comradeship.

There are events which were part of a program for this entity only in that they were possibility/probability vortices having to do with your societal culture. These events include the nature of the living or standard of living, the type of relationships entered into in your legal framework, and the social climate during the incarnation. The incarnation was understood to be one which would take place at harvest.

These givens, shall we say, apply to millions of your peoples. Those aware of evolution and desirous in the very extreme of attaining the heart of love and the radiance which gives understanding no matter what the lessons programmed: they have to do with other-selves, not with events; they have to do with giving, not receiving, for the lessons of love are of this nature both for positive and negative. Those negatively harvestable will be found at this time endeavoring to share their love of self.

There are those whose lessons are more random due to their present inability to comprehend the nature and mechanism of the evolution of mind, body, and spirit. Of these we may say that the process is guarded by those who never cease their watchful expectation of being of service. There is no entity without help, either through self-awareness of the unity of creation or through guardians of the self which protect the less sophisticated mind/body/spirit from any permanent separation from unity while the lessons of your density continue.

QUESTIONER: Could you give an example of negative polarization sharing love of self? It would seem to me that that would deplete negative polarization. Could you expand on the concept?

RA: I am Ra. We may not use examples of known beings due to the infringement this would cause. Thus we must be general.

The negatively oriented being will be one who feels that it has found power that gives meaning to its existence precisely as the positive polarization does feel. This negative entity will strive to offer these understandings to other-selves, most usually by the process of forming the elite, the disciples, and teaching the need and rightness of the enslavement of other-selves for their own good. These other-selves are conceived to be dependent upon the self and in need of the guidance and the wisdom of the self.

QUESTIONER: Thank you. How does the ability to hold visual images in mind allow the adept to do polarization in consciousness without external action?

RA: I am Ra. This is not a simple query, for the adept is one which will go beyond the green ray which signals entry into harvestability. The adept will not simply be tapping into intelligent energy as a means of readiness for harvest but tapping into both intelligent energy and intelligent infinity for the purpose of transmuting planetary harvestability and consciousness.

The means of this working lie within. The key is first, silence, and secondly, singleness of thought. Thusly a visualization which can be held steady to the inward eye for several of your minutes, as you measure time, will signal the adept's increase in singleness of thought. This singleness of thought then can be used by the positive adept to work in group ritual visualizations for the raising of positive energy, by negative adepts for the increase in personal power.

QUESTIONER: Can you tell me what the adept, after being able to hold the image for several minutes, does to affect planetary consciousness or affect positive polarity?

RA: I am Ra. When the positive adept touches intelligent infinity from within, this is the most powerful of connections for it is the connection of the whole mind/body/spirit complex microcosm with the macrocosm. This connection enables the, shall we say, green-ray true color in time/space to manifest in your space/time. In green ray thoughts are beings. In your illusion this is normally not so.

The adepts then become living channels for love and light and are able to channel this radiance directly into the planetary web of energy nexi. The ritual will always end by the grounding of this energy in praise and thanksgiving and the release of this energy into the planetary whole.

QUESTIONER: Could you give me more information on the energy fields of the body as related to the right and left brain and if this is somehow related to the pyramid shape as far as energy focusing goes?

I am at a loss as to how to get into this line of questioning, so I will ask that question.

RA: I am Ra. We are similarly at a loss at this line of answering. We may say that the pyramid shape is but one which focuses the instreamings of energy for use by entities which may become aware of these instreamings. We may say further that the shape of your physical brain is not significant as a shape for concentrating instreamings of energy. Please ask more specifically if you may that which you seek.

QUESTIONER: Each of us feels, in meditation, energy upon the head in various places. Could you tell me what this is, what it signifies, and what the various places in which we feel it signify?

RA: I am Ra. Forgetting the pyramid will be of aid to you in the study of these experiences.

The instreamings of energy are felt by the energy centers which need, and are prepared for, activation. Thus those who feel the stimulation at violet-ray level are getting just that. Those feeling it within the forehead between the brows are experiencing indigo ray and so forth. Those experiencing tingling and visual images are having some blockage in the energy center being activated and thus the electrical body spreads this energy out and its effect is diffused.

Those not truly sincerely requesting this energy may yet feel it if the entities are not well trained in psychic defense. Those not desirous of experiencing these sensations and activations and changes even upon the subconscious level will not experience anything due to their abilities at defense and armoring against change.

QUESTIONER: Is it normal to get two simultaneous stimulations at once?

RA: I am Ra. The most normal for the adept is the following: the indigo stimulation activating that great gateway into healing, magical work, prayerful attention, and the radiance of being; and the stimulation of the violet ray which is the spiritual giving and taking from and to Creator, from Creator to Creator.

This is a desirable configuration.

Please ask one more full query at this working.

QUESTIONER: Can you expand on the concept which is that it is necessary for an entity, during incarnation in the physical as we know it, to become polarized or interact properly with other entities and why this isn't possible in between incarnations when the entity is aware of what he wants to do. Why must he come into an incarnation and lose conscious memory of what he wants to do and then act in a way in which he hopes to act?

RA: I am Ra. Let us give the example of the man who sees all the poker hands. He then knows the game. It is but child's play to gamble, for it is no risk. The other hands are known. The possibilities are known and the hand will be played correctly but with no interest.

In time/space and in the true color green density, the hands of all are open to the eye. The thoughts, the feelings, the troubles, all these may be seen. There is no deception and no desire for deception. Thus much may be accomplished in harmony but the mind/body/spirit gains little polarity from this interaction.

Let us re-examine this metaphor and multiply it into the longest poker game you can imagine, a lifetime. The cards are love, dislike, limitation, unhappiness, pleasure, etc. They are dealt and re-dealt and re-dealt continuously. You may, during this incarnation begin—and we stress begin—to know your own cards. You may begin to find the love within you. You may begin to balance your pleasure, your limitations, etc. However, your only indication of other-selves' cards is to look into the eyes.

You cannot remember your hand, their hands, perhaps even the rules of this game. This game can only be won by those who lose their cards in the melting influence of love, can only be won by those who lay their pleasures, their limitations, their all upon the table face up and say inwardly: "All, all of you players, each other-self, whatever your hand, I love you." This is the game: to know, to accept, to forgive, to balance, and to open the self in love. This cannot be done without the forgetting, for it would carry no weight in the life of the mind/body/spirit beingness totality.

Is there a brief query before we leave this instrument?

QUESTIONER: Is there anything that we can do to make the instrument more comfortable or to improve the contact?

RA: I am Ra. You are conscientious and your alignments are careful. It would be well to take care that this instrument's neck is placed carefully upon its support.

I am Ra. I leave you, my friends, in the love and the light of the One Infinite Creator. Go forth, then, rejoicing in the power and in the peace of the One Infinite Creator. Adonai.

INDEX

ABOUT THE AUTHORS

DON ELKINS was born in Louisville, Kentucky, in 1930. He held a BS and MS in mechanical engineering from the University of Louisville, as well as an MS in general engineering from Speed Scientific School. He was professor of physics and engineering at the University of Louisville for twelve years from 1953 to 1965. In 1965 he left his tenured position and became a Boeing 727 pilot for a major airline to devote himself more fully to UFO and paranormal research. He also served with distinction in the US Army as a master sergeant during the Korean War.

Don Elkins began his research into the paranormal in 1955. In 1962, Don started an experiment in channeling, using the protocols he had learned from a contactee group in Detroit, Michigan. That experiment blossomed into a channeling practice that led eventually to the Law of One material 19 years later. Don passed away on November 7, 1984.

CARLA L. RUECKERT (McCarty) was born in 1943 in Lake Forest, Illinois. She completed undergraduate studies in English literature at the University of Louisville in 1966 and earned her master's degree in library service in 1971.

Carla became partners with Don in 1968. In 1970, they formed L/L Research. In 1974, she began channeling and continued in that effort until she was stopped in 2011 by a spinal fusion surgery. During four of those thirty-seven years of channeling (1981–1984), Carla served as the instrument for the Law of One material.

In 1987, she married Jim McCarty, and together they continued the mission of L/L Research. Carla passed into larger life on April 1, 2015.

JAMES McCARTY was born in 1947 in Kearney, Nebraska. After receiving an undergraduate degrees from the University of Nebraska at Kearney and a master of science in early childhood education from the University of Florida, Jim moved to a piece of wilderness in Marion County, Kentucky, in 1974 to build his own log cabin in the woods, and to develop a self-sufficient lifestyle. For the next six years, he was in almost complete retreat.

He founded the Rock Creek Research and Development Laboratories in 1977 to further his teaching efforts. After experimenting, Jim decided that he preferred the methods and directions he had found in studying with L/L Research in 1978. In 1980, he joined his research with Don's and Carla's.

Jim and Carla were married in 1987. Jim has a wide L/L correspondence and creates wonderful gardens and stonework. He enjoys beauty, nature, dance, and silence.

NOTE: The Ra contact continued until session number 106. There are five volumes total in The Law of One series, Book I–Book V. There is also other material available from our research group on our archive website, www.llresearch.org.

You may reach us by email at contact@llresearch.org, or by mail at: L/L Research, P.O. Box 5195, Louisville, KY 40255-0195

NOTES